Footprint Handbook
Reykjavík

LAURA DIXON

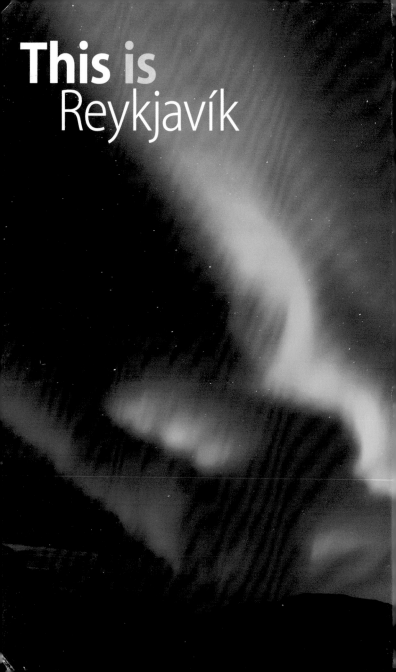

This is
Reykjavík

I had been dreaming about visiting Reykjavík for years before I finally made my first trip to Iceland. But even in my wildest dreams, I could not have conjured it up. It is, to repeat a tired cliché, fire and ice; it is light and dark, sometimes most unexpectedly; it is hot and cold, again, not always when you think it will be; and wild and windy and wonderful, and is somewhere I still dream about today.

Your challenge is to fit in as many Icelandic expériences as you can on your trip. Drink in the clearest air in the world, the bright light and the fresh mountain stream water. Try the extremes of cuisine – from contemporary New Nordic delights to the ancient Icelandic delicacies of sheep's head and dried fish.

Watch children feeding geese at the town pond, encounter a real-life Viking longhouse under the street and drink coffee in the many cafés. Reykjavík is perfectly positioned for a city/country break, as you can drive just half an hour from the city to watch the Northern Lights in winter, because of the lack of light pollution, and just a bit further to walk the fault line in Þingvellir National Park, where the American and Eurasian tectonic plates are pulling apart.

Skidoo on a glacier, ride an Icelandic pony through lava fields, meet a stuffed polar bear and watch icebergs dance on an inland lake. Retreat to a hotel beside ancient volcanoes where seals play by the shore and a cone-shaped glacier nearby is said to have mystical powers. Drink in the midnight sun and party till the morning. Swim in thermal pools, buy a *lopipeysa* and take the best photographs of your life. Then book your next trip back. That's how I would do it.

Laura Dixon

Best of
Reykjavík

❶ 871 +/-2 The Settlement Exhibition

Based around a 10th-century longhouse that was discovered beneath the streets of the city in 2001, this is perhaps Reykjavík's most exciting museum. Combining carefully preserved archaeological finds with high-tech interactive displays, it captures the imagination and brings the world of the Vikings to life. Page 20.

❷ National Museum of Iceland

Tangible exhibitions and multimedia displays provide a fascinating insight into 1200 years of Icelandic history and culture, from the Settlement Era through to independence. Featuring everyday objects such as swords, drinking horns and children's toys made from whale bone, it's not glitzy but gives a genuine feel for the country's heritage. Page 24.

❸ Blue Lagoon

The world-famous Blue Lagoon is a steaming pool of opaque turquoise water that leaches minerals from the lava bed, filling it with healing properties. Here you can lie back and relax, put a mud pack on your face … and try not to let that whiff of sulphur put you off. Page 64.

❻ West Fjords

Arguably the most breathtaking scenery in the country is to be found in the far northwest. Connected to the mainland by a 7-km strip of land, the remote West Fjords are stunningly beautiful with amazing coastal walks, tiny fishing villages nestled against precipitous mountains and literally millions of breeding seabirds. Page 76.

❹ Þingvellir National Park

Dramatically set on a fissure of the North Atlantic Ridge, at Þingvellir you can actually see the Eurasian and American continental plates drawing apart. The extraordinary landscape of Iceland's first parliament can be explored on horseback, on foot or by venturing into the subterranean world by diving to the Silfra Rift or hiking through lava tunnels. Page 66.

❺ Snæfellsnes Peninsula

Topped with a cone-shaped glacier immortalized in Jules Verne *Journey to the Centre of the Earth*, Snæfellsnes is one of Iceland's most accessible hiking destinations. Dramatic cliffs, lava fields and golden sands make up the diverse landscape of this 100-km peninsula, which is home to an impressive array of birdlife. Page 74.

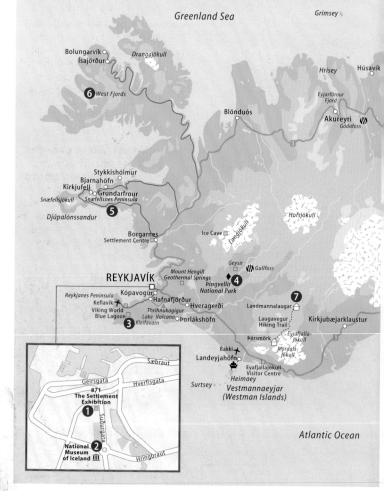

Greenland Sea

Grímsey

Bolungarvík
Ísafjörður

Drangajökull

Hrísey   Húsavík

6 *West Fjords*

Eyjarförður Fjord

Blönduós

Akureyri
Goðafoss

Stykkishólmur
Bjarnahöfn
Kirkjufell
Grundarfrour
Snæfellsjökull *Snæfellsnes Peninsula*
5

Hofsjökull

Djúpalónssandur

Langjökull

Borgarnes
Settlement Centre

Ice Cave

REYKJAVÍK

Geysir   *Gullfoss*

Mount Hengill
Geothermal Springs
Þingvellir
National Park   **4**

Reykjanes Peninsula   Kópavogur
Keflavík
Viking World   Hafnarfjörður
Blue Lagoon   *Þríhnúkagígur*   Hveragerði
3 *Lake Volcano*   Þorlákshöfn
Kleifavatn

Landmannalaugar   **7**

Kirkjubæjarklaustur

Laugavegur
Hiking Trail
Þórsmörk   *Eyjafjalla-
jökull*

Bakki   *Mýrdals-
jökull*
Landeyjahöfn

Eyjafjallajökull
Visitor Centre
Surtsey   *Heimaey*
**Vestmannaeyjar
(Westman Islands)**

Atlantic Ocean

Geirsgata
871
**The Settlement
Exhibition**
1

Sæbraut

Hverfisgata

Sölugata

**National
Museum
of Iceland**
2

Hringbraut

❼ Landmannalaugar

An area of outstanding natural beauty in the central highlands, Landmannalaugar is the start point for one of Iceland's most spectacular hikes. Take an outdoor bath in a natural hot spring surrounded by multicoloured rhyolite mountains or trek through rugged lava fields and shiny obsidian to the lush forests of Þórsmörk. Page 79.

❽ Jökulsárlón

This stunning glacial lagoon in the far southeast of Iceland has been used as the backdrop for a number of action movies and it's easy to see why. Pale blue floating icebergs contrast dramatically with the black sand and brooding volcanic mountains. Explore it by boat or snowmobile but don't forget your camera. Page 82.

❾ Lake Mývatn

Northern Iceland's undisputed drawcard is unlike anywhere else in the country. Violent geological activity has produced a weird and wonderful landscape of desolate craters, bubbling mud pots and geothermal caves. Dotted with islands, the shallow lake and surrounding wetlands attract an exceptionally large variety of waterbirds. Page 93.

Atlantic puffins on Látrabjarg cliffs

When to go

...and when not to

Being so far north, travel in Iceland is highly seasonal due to the extremes of temperatures and daylight hours. Visit November to February to see the Northern Lights or late June to August to experience the midnight sun. Hours of daylight shape how you can see the country: in mid-December there are around four hours of daylight, while in mid-July there is approximately one hour of darkness and 23 hours of daylight.

The shoulder seasons of spring and autumn are good for walking and activities, and are cheaper than the peak summer season; winter is the low season for accommodation and flights, excluding the Christmas/New Year period.

Whenever you visit you need to pack warm clothes because conditions can change quickly. The changing weather is one of the few hazards in the country and to help you plan activities such as glacier climbing, hiking and cycling, it's a good idea to visit the website www.safetravel.is, which has kit lists, driving information and everything outdoorsy people need to know about visiting the country.

Note that in the winter months many routes to the centre of Iceland and its Highlands are closed and don't reopen until the late spring. This might affect you if you plan to visit Landmannalaugar or do the Laugavegurinn hike, for example (see page 79).

Weather Reykjavík

January	February	March	April	May	June
4°C -2°C 68mm	3°C -3°C 78mm	4°C -2°C 94mm	6°C 1°C 39mm	10°C 4°C 35mm	13°C 7°C 21mm

July	August	September	October	November	December
14°C 9°C 26mm	14°C 8°C 31mm	11°C 6°C 41mm	8°C 3°C 26mm	5°C 0°C 59mm	4°C -2°C 60mm

What to do

activities from glacier hiking to soaking in the Blue Lagoon

Caving

Þingvellir National Park has numerous lava caves beneath it. Trips can be arranged from Reykjavik to visit the lava caves and tubes from eruptions that took place 9000 years ago.

Diving

The Silfra Rift in Þingvellir Lake is a unique place for diving. The clear water means excellent visibility and you can dive right down to where bubbles of water show that the tectonic plates are moving away.

Dog sledding

Dog sledding can take place all year round depending on the snow; trips are conducted on glaciers in the summer, meaning a longer ride from Reykjavík, and closer to the city at other times.

Fishing

Iceland's lakes and rivers are populated with trout and salmon. The season runs Apr-Sep. Salmon fishing needs to be booked long in advance but trout-fishing permits are available at short notice. The most popular areas are Reykjavík, Snæfellsnes Peninsula, Landmannalaugar and Akureyri.

Glacier tours

Snowmobile and snow cat tours of Snæfellsjökull glacier run from the town of Arnastapi on the south coast of Snæfellsnes, plus guided drives on to the snow. See page 79.

Hiking

There are a number of hiking routes in Þingvellir around the ancient assembly site and nearby abandoned farms. The visitor centre has a park ranger who can offer information in the summer, otherwise many of the hikes can be tackled independently.

Iceland's best hot springs

Laugardalslaug Thermal Pool and Spa, see page 31
Blue Lagoon, see page 64
Geysir, see page 68
Landmannalaugar, see page 79
Mount Hengill Geothermal Springs, see page 81
Lake Mývatn Nature Baths, see page 93

ON THE ROAD

In search of the Northern Lights

Iceland has plenty of extraordinary natural wonders and one of the very best is the Northern Lights or aurora borealis. Because the city of Reykjavík is so small and offers very little in the way of light pollution, it is possible to see them on a clear night just half an hour from the city. The season for Northern Light watching is late October to March, and evenings are given a grading according to how likely it is to see them, with a cold clear night in spring or autumn given the highest rating. Cloudy nights offer very little chance of seeing this natural phenomenon.

These greenish, yellowish, pinkish stripes in the sky are caused by electrically charged particles emitted by the sun that interact with the earth's magnetic field. It makes no difference if you're viewing them from a mountain or a valley because they are so high up in the earth's atmosphere. They also don't make a sound. As the particles collide with the upper atmosphere at great speeds, they cause the air to glow in the beautiful auroral colours.

Intensity is extremely variable, and is affected by solar activity. This peaks in 11-year cycles. The last peak, or solar maximum, was in 2013, when large sunspots appeared on the sun and its irradiant output was increased. The Northern Lights were particularly intense around this time and will be brighter than normal for the following few years.

In Iceland, the brightest aurora are in the spring and autumn rather than midwinter, although then can be seen at any time between October and March, and the best time to look is between 2100 and 2400. What you need to look for is a shadowy grey bow shape in the sky, rather like the shape of a rainbow but in a cloudy grey colour. It splits gradually into lines and soon green and pink lights which dance across the sky. This display can last for a few hours or disappear within 10 minutes. If you plan to photograph them, be sure to use a slow shutter speed and no flash. Colours are far more intense seen through a lens than in the sky with the naked eye.

The best places to see the Northern Lights are a little out of the city, although they can still be seen in a brightly lit street. About 10 km from Reykjavík, Heiðmörk is a good place that is far away from artificial light pollution, as is Nesjavallavegur, 20 km away. If you have the chance to stay outside the city, **Hotel Ranga** in South Iceland has well positioned hot tubs for Northern Light viewing, and **Hotel Buðir** on the Snæfellsnes Peninsula is a wonderful wilderness location with a great record of offering views of them. Many Reykjavík-based tour companies offering trips to see the Northern Lights by bus and even on horseback (see page 60).

There are plenty of strange traditions about the Northern Lights. The Japanese believe that conceiving a baby under them will produce a child of extreme intelligence, while Icelanders believe that watching the Northern Lights while pregnant will make your baby cross-eyed.

Wildlife watching in Iceland

Depending on the time of year, you can see puffins and whales on boat trips from Reykjavík harbour, and also from various places around Iceland. Bird watchers might like to make a special trip to Þingvellir to watch birds from North America and Europe.

Puffin watching

The best time to watch puffins is between June and early August each year. Puffins migrate at the end of August each year, along with their pufflings, or chicks. They are a common bird in Iceland and are the size of small penguins with brightly coloured parrot beaks. They are as eccentric as the country, live in burrow like rabbits and can dive up to 18 m under water to catch their food, the sand eel. They are nicknamed the *profastur* – meaning professors – for their dinner-jacketed appearance.

Summer whale-watching trips from Reykjavík often include a chance to see these sea birds, which congregate around Lundey island in the harbour, which takes its name from the Icelandic name for puffin.

Puffins are hunted in the Westman Islands and other coastal spots around the country by men wielding butterfly nets. Most of the cliffs have an immense number of seabirds and the most tricky to access are hunted by

Iceland's most famous hike is the 4-day (55-km) Laugavegurinn, between the volcanic landscape of Landmannalaugar and the forest of Þorsmörk. Passing glaciers, mountains, gorges and geothermal springs, there are also a number of rivers to cross en route. See page 79 for further details.

Horse riding

Icelandic ponies are not only loveable shaggy beast but have a special talent: they can run in 5 gears, rather than the standard 4. Most horses can walk, trot, canter and run, but Icelandic ponies can also *tölt* – they run with both legs from the same side of the body at the same time. It's a curious trick. The ponies themselves are pure bred and hardy and were brought over at the time of the Vikings. Local riding stables near the city offer day and half-day tours, but there are also opportunities on the Snaefellsnes Peninsula, Landmmanalaugar and Akureyri.

Northern Lights

Many hotels and hostels can arrange Northern Lights tours. The best time to see them is Nov-Feb. Most companies offer a free trip if you fail to see them on your first outing – sightings are not guaranteed as they are heavily weather dependent.

men on ropes, rappelling around the cliffs. Seabirds eggs are also collected and you'll find puffin and guillemot among the native dishes on traditional restaurants' menus everywhere in the country. Because puffins are only really in season during the summer, the freshest tasting and best are on menus then, not in the winter. See below for puffin watching tours from Reykjavík, and page 85 for information on the Westman Islands' annual Puffin Festival.

Whale watching

Reykjavík's harbour has plenty of opportunities for whale watching. The best time to watch migratory whales in Iceland is May to September, but there are whales in the water around the country all year round. There are 23 types of whale that you could see, including minke, humpback, blue and orca, with minke the most common species sighted. There's also a high chance of spotting harbour porpoise and white beaked dolphin on a whale-watching tour. Be sure to wrap up warm as the Arctic wind is very cold; if you think you might be seasick, the whale-watching company can supply seasickness remedies.

The best place in the country to see whales is Húsavík, a town in northern Iceland. There is a good whale-watching centre in the town (see page 100). Iceland no longer whales commercially, but does hunt a small quota of whales for scientific purposes every year. To find out more about the Icelandic whaling industry and about whales in Iceland in general, visit www.icewhale. is. See page 61 for tour companies offering whale watching from Reykjavík.

Skiing

Iceland isn't a place you'd visit just for the skiing, but it does have some decent slopes with ski areas just 25 mins from Reykjavík. Húsavík offers cross-country skiing, while Akureyri is a popular base for both downhill and heli-skiing.

Swimming

The country's most famous natural swimming pool is the iconic Blue Lagoon; what most people don't know is that within the city there are a number of great geothermal swimming pools for a fraction of the price. Also, in Reykjavík is the quirky Nauthólsvík Beach where the sea is pumped with geothermal water.

The Lake Mývatn Nature Baths near Húsavík are known as the 'blue lagoon of the north'.

Whitewater rafting and kayaking

Rivers accessible from Reykjavík for whitewater rafting are mainly a drive away in the south of Iceland where there are a number of different levels at which to raft. Most of the activity-based tour operators can organize rafting and kayking.

Where to stay

from city chic to hikers' huts

Let's get this straight from the start: accommodation in Reykjavík isn't cheap and isn't pretty. As a capital city, it has the full range of business hotels, boutique hotels, chain hotels and apartments and B&Bs, along with some excellent youth hostels. But you'll notice that prices are above average, particularly in the summer months, and it's a good idea to book in advance, search the web for deals and keep an eye out for special offers. Companies such as **Airbnb** ⓘ *www.airbnb. co.uk*, can help find good-value accommodation and connect with hosts directly.

Reykjavík's architecture isn't as fairytale twee as Copenhagen, nor as stylish and classical as Stockholm; instead it's a little bit more Soviet bloc. Stylish boutique hotels are clad in grey concrete slabs, mainly because the weather can be brutal, but also because, until fairly recently, Reykjavík was little more than a village and the city as it is today has grown up fairly quickly, so there is little sense of historical architecture. When you choose your hotel, don't judge the book by its cover.

The best place to stay is in the 101 district, or Old Town; the Laugardalur Valley, 3 km away, is also a good option. Any further out and you'll need a car or public transport to experience the city and its attractions. There are also some notable hotels beyond the city in Mosfellsbaer and Snæfellsnes that are worth booking for a night or so for a true Icelandic wilderness experience.

The city's **youth hostels** are a really good bet – you can stay in a private room, family room or dorm – especially if you're on a budget or travelling solo. **Hostelling**

Price codes

Where to stay	Restaurants
€€€€ over €300	€€€ over €30
€€€ €200-300	€€ €15-30
€€ €100-200	€ under €15
€ under €100	

Based on the cost of two people sharing a double room in high season.

Price refers to the cost of a two-course meal for one person, including drinks and service charge.

Five of the strangest specialities

Cod chins or cheeks You might think this is a mistranslation when you see it on the menu, but the Icelanders often prefer to eat the meat from cod heads than the more traditional fillets. It's a delicacy and certainly nicer than sheep's head, also a national dish, originating from the days when it was necessary to eat everything available to stay alive.

Hákarl This delight is Greenland shark cured by being left underground for three months, then dug up when it is lightly rotten to be served cubed as a starter. The taste stays with you for far longer than you'd want, and the best way of losing it is by necking a shot of *brennivín*. Try it at Kolaportið market (see page 29).

Pickled ram's testicles Often served pressed into a cake with garlic, as a jam or as a kind of pâté. It doesn't taste too bad if you don't think about it too much, particularly in the pâté form.

Pylsur Not so much weird as weirdly popular, Icelandic hot dogs are a national dish of their own, frankfurter sausages smothered in mustard, ketchup, onions and anything else the vendor can get his hands on. They all taste very similar, but Bæjarins Beztu Pylsur on Tryggvagata is reputedly the best.

Seabirds Take your pick from smoked puffin, guillemot and boiled fulmar's eggs – they have a slight oily flavour but can be delicious, especially as a starter. Beware if you're thinking of buying eggs from the market to cook yourself, though, as it's common for seabirds' eggs to contain half-hatched chicks.

International runs hostels across the country and membership to it can offer reduced rates. There are also a handful of hostels run by individuals, including one in an old biscuit factory owned by a group of Premiership footballers.

Camping is also an option, in the Reykjavík Campsite, 3 km from the city centre, and Icelandic B&Bs offer sleeping bag accommodation in the summer, where you get a bed for the night but don't pay for linens, making it a little cheaper.

For a chance to live like a local, there are some ultra-trendy self-catering apartments in the city, with top-of-the-range fixtures and fittings and high prices to match. You can also stay in a couple of traditional Icelandic corrugated iron-clad cottages in the Old Town, which have a charming feel to them. Farmstay accommodation not far from the city is a popular family choice.

Accommodation prices drop in September; the peak months are June to August. If you visit in the summer, most hotels and B&Bs have thick blinds to keep out the midnight sun (it's light for most of the night) but it's a good idea to bring an eye mask if you have one. If you are staying anywhere in the 101 district over a Friday or Saturday night, you might also like to bring earplugs as the noise from very late nightlife can be disruptive.

Food
& drink

from lobster soup to pickled ram's testicles

Reykjavík's restaurants have embraced the New Nordic cuisine trend and serve some of the most delicious delicate flavours drawing on the natural bounty provided: free-range lamb, salmon from fine clear rivers, lobster and langoustine, and the likes of wild Icelandic moss and wild herbs. Restaurants such as **Vox** and **Dill** are champions of this approach and bring a uniquely Icelandic flavour to the trend by focusing on Icelandic lamb in particular.

Eating out in Reykjavík is not all about tiny portions, flavoured foam and concept dining, however. The city has plenty to offer in all price brackets, from a cheap on-street *pylsur* (hot dog) or a fisherman's shack selling lobster soup to ultra-high end white table-clothed restaurants. There is a diverse array of restaurants which you might not expect from such a small city. You can certainly find Chinese, Indian, Thai and Mexican food alongside more classical Icelandic restaurants and bars, bistros and cafés. One thing that may be harder to find is an early breakfast: before 0800 you may have to visit a hotel to be fed. The city's finest hotels are all prime locations for upmarket bars and restaurants too.

Fish, of course, is a mainstay of Icelandic cuisine and is abundant in the waters around it. It doesn't get much fresher than this – Reykjavík's harbour is only a few kilometers from the centre. Traditional cod soup – creamy broth with a piece of cod in the centre – comes highly recommended, as does lobster soup. There is a terrific Icelandic fish and chips joint by the old harbour that plays on the English tradition to great effect.

And then there are the more dubious pleasures of traditional, historical Icelandic cuisine. A cursory glance at the traditional food eaten in the country looks like a serious challenge for *Man vs Food*: boiled sheep's head, pickled ram's testicles, rotten shark, wind-dried fish, puffin, seabird's egg and whale. Gordon Ramsay famously had a hard time keeping the rotten shark down. These dubious delicacies date back to the time of subsistence farming in Iceland when nobody had a fridge; novel methods, mainly involving curd, were used to preserve the scanty food found on the island during the winter.

Today you can try them at various tourist-orientated restaurants around the town centre and in the **Kolaportið** market at the weekend. Icelanders sit down to a traditional meal of these delights one night of the year at **Thorrablot**, the winter feast, but for all other days of the year eat like the rest of us. Puffin is a summer dish and has a rich, gamey flavour and is worth trying; the others may be left alone, depending on how adventurous you are. Whale has been eaten in the country but is now only found on select menus and is frowned upon by numerous animal rights agencies.

Traditional Icelandic snacks include licorice, *skyr* (a thick yoghurt), and wind-dried fish, bought in bags like crisps.

Eating out in general is expensive; going self-catering can help to cut the costs, but of course is less fun. Buying Icelandic rather than recognizable international brands, can keep costs lower. Restaurants tend to open for lunch at 1300 and for dinner at 1800. Note that service charges and VAT are usually included in prices and that tipping is not done here.

Drink

Alcohol is expensive in bars and restaurants and is also available in state controlled off-licenses called *vinbuðin*. It is highly taxed; bringing alcohol into the country via duty free is a cheaper way to do it.

The country's unique spirit, *brennivin*, is made from potato mash and flavoured with caraway seeds and is known as the Black Death. It tastes a little like vodka with a more powerful kick, and is a good combination with *hakarl*, or rotten shark (or at least can take the edge off its flavour). At 37.5%, it will give you a hangover to remember.

Icelandic bars range from small and cosy pubs, where everyone will look at you when you walk in, to large and expansive Irish pubs, licensed coffee shops and chic cocktail bars in many of the high-end hotels. Naturally very reticent as people, Icelanders can become friendly and voluble after a drink. There are over a hundred bars in Reykjavík, some which turn into clubs later on. Fashions turn on a sixpence here, however, so what was hot yesterday might be deemed dull tomorrow; if your bar is empty but next door is busy, follow the crowds for a great night out. It is not uncommon to return home at 0700 from a bar or club in high summer; closing hours are negotiable. As with most of Europe, excluding the UK, nightlife doesn't really get going until after midnight.

Café society is alive and well in the city. Reykjavík is teeming with independent coffee shops – you won't see a Starbucks here. Instead, cafés are lovely cosy havens where you can buy a large pot of coffee for a handful of coins and sit and check out the bizarre fashions or unusual music going on around you. Cafés tend to open from 1000 and often double up as bars in the evening, opening to around 0100 or whenever it gets quiet, with later opening hours on a Friday or Saturday night.

Essential Reykjavík

Finding your feet

Iceland's main international airport is at Keflavik, a 50-minute drive west of Reykjavík. Airport buses meet international flights and take a full coach load of people to a central hub in Reykjavík before dropping them at their hotels in a minibus or van. Return tickets cost ISK 4400 and the key operators are **Flybus**, www.re.is/flybus, and **Airport Express**, www.airportexpress.is. Alternatively, there is a taxi rank outside Arrivals; the average price for one to four people is around ISK 16,500.

Getting around

Downtown Reykjavik is compact and easily manageable on foot or by bicycle.

Best free things to do

- Visit the **Pearl** and take in the view over the city from the viewing platform.
- Admire the architecture of the mighty **Hallgrímskirkja church** from inside and out.
- Be a culture vulture and visit the **Nordic House**, **City Hall** and **Harpa** buildings.
- Climb **Mount Esja**, a short distance from the city.
- Wander around **Kolaportið Flea Market** and sample some Icelandic delicacies, such as rotten shark.
- Walk along the harbour to the **Sólfar Viking boat sculpture**, or in the other direction to the lighthouse and Grótta Beach.
- Take a **free walking tour**, http://citywalk.is.
- Look up at the sky: at the right time of year, you might catch a glimpse of the **Northern Lights**.

The city has an extensive network of local buses running out to the suburbs.

When to go

The peak season is June to August and many attractions close outside these months and buses may run limited services. However, visitors will still find plenty to do in the colder months with activities such as spa breaks, backcountry skiing, glacier snowmobiling and Northern Lights, becoming ever more popular. Prices drop significantly off season.

Reykjavík Welcome Card

The tourist offices, along with other major cultural institutions in the city, sell the **Reykjavík Welcome Card**, www.visitreykjavik.is/travel/reykjavik-city-card. It's available for 24, 48 and 72 hours and gives free admission to the city's thermal pools, many of its museums and attractions, unlimited bus travel and discounts at shops and restaurants. It costs ISK 3300 for 24 hours, ISK 4400 for 48 hours and ISK 4900 for 72 hours. Thermal pools only cost around ISK 650 to enter but it offers a significant saving if you want to visit most of the major art galleries and museums, which can cost ISK 1400 each. Card holders can also get free internet access at the tourist information office on Aðalstræti.

Time required

Half a day to see the main sights and get a feel for the town. Three or four days to explore the museums and galleries at a relaxed pace.

Reykjavík

Iceland's capital was founded by the Vikings in AD 874, drawn by the smoke from its hot springs. The name 'Reykjavík' means smoky bay and those springs today are still in use, heating the city's water along with its swimming pools.

Reykjavík isn't a classically beautiful city and its suburbs in particular are singularly grey and concrete. What draws the eye, however, are the colourful cottages in the centre, and the looming shape of Mount Esja across the bay. This mountain is known for its changing colours and shape – watch it for half an hour and you'll see why.

Reykjavík's population is around that of Chester in the UK, at 120,000, and swells so much due to tourism that a politician once suggested that tourist numbers should be curbed. Fortunately for all of us, he was loudly shouted down.

You'll notice as soon as you arrive that Reykjavík, although a capital, is not a big city. You can easily walk the characterful centre in half a day, taking in its key cultural attractions, from the harbour village to the town hall, parliament and museums.

The Old Town of Reykjavík, or 101 Reykjavík, includes the harbour and is the main area for restaurants, bars and shopping in the centre of the city. It has colourful corrugated-iron-clad houses, museums and the town pond. The sights are worth exploring and the walk along the harbour is beautiful. Alternatively, you can soak up the atmosphere of the city in the small cafés and hot pots of Reykjavík's seven swimming pools.

Austurvöllur Square

This square is the real heart of the city. The name means 'east field' and was originally at least six times bigger than it is today. Farmers riding into the city for business left their horses at Lækjartorg Square to camp in the area. Today, it's still a grassy square, in front of the Alþing (Parliament House), surrounded by bars and cafés and overlooked by the rather stern-looking statue of Jón Sigurdsson. He's a national hero, a politician who led the 19th-century movement towards independence from Denmark. When it finally came in 1944, it was decided that his birthday, 17 June, should be celebrated as the National Day. In the corner of the square is a small church, which is actually the city cathedral, built 1787-1796 and enlarged in the mid-18th century. It's not as grand or forbidding as Hallgrímskirkja on the hill above the city but is nevertheless an important ecclesiastical building.

Also in the square is **Hotel Borg**, a graceful white art-deco hotel overlooking the square (see page 39). This was Iceland's first luxury hotel and deserves a look round for the architecture, well-preserved rooms and sense of grandeur. You can see why Marlene Dietrich stayed here in 1944.

★871+/- 2 The Settlement Exhibition

Aðalstræti 16, T411 6300, www.reykjavikmuseum.is. Jun-Aug daily 0900-2000. Settlement Exhibition ISK 1400, settlement sagas ISK 1000, combined ticket ISK 2200, under 18s free. Free with Reykjavík Welcome Card.

Aðalstræti is the oldest street in Reykjavík and on its corner, under **Hotel Centrum**, you can find this captivating exhibition all about the settlement of the city. While excavating the site for the hotel in 2001, archaeological remains were found, which turned out to be the oldest relics of human habitation in Reykjavík, dating to AD 871 +/- two years. The finds include a hall or longhouse from the 10th century which is preserved for visitors today. It is surrounded by an interactive exhibition showing Reykjavík as the wooded valley it was at the time, and describing the daily life of those who lived here. It's a wonderful introduction to the city's history with insights into the lifestyle of the first settlers and artefacts from central Reykjavík excavations on display. Computer generated imagery gives an idea about how the buildings were constructed.

As of 2015, Iceland's precious **settlement sagas** have been on display in a new exhibition here. The medieval manuscripts are the richest evidence on the culture and mentalities of Northern Europeans in pagan times and represent the cornerstone of Icelandic history, genealogy and culture. They are displayed in near darkness to prevent any damage to the 1000-year-old calfskins on which they're written.

The museum shop sells quirky gifts including guillemot-shaped candles, whale bone toys based on an old Viking design and t-shirts. If you are interested in Viking history and only have a chance to visit one museum, make it this one.

Tjörnin

The town pond, Tjörnin, is popular with young and old alike and frequently has a cluster of children round it feeding the ducks and greylag geese. It freezes in winter and children and adults alike skate, walk and wander on it. It was created millions of years ago at the end of the last ice age as a sand and gravel bar was built up by the pounding waves of Faxaflói Bay.

City Hall (Ráðhús)

Tjarnargata 11, T411 111, www.visitreykjavik.is/reykjavik-city-hall. Year round Mon-Fri 0800-1900, Sat-Sun 1200-1800. Free. Café daily 1200-1330, snacks from around ISK 650.

The modern building, which seems to rise out of the water, was designed in 1987 as the result of a national competition. It stands right on the edge of the pond with a footbridge leading across into it. Inside, the second and third floors are reserved for the city council, while the first floor is open to visitors and designed to be an extension of the streets outside. Here you'll find a large relief map of Iceland, a small tourist information centre and a café serving drinks, soup and sandwiches.

National Gallery of Iceland (Listasafn)

Fríkirkjuvegur 7, east side of the pond, T515 9600, www.listasafn.is. Mid-May to mid-Sep Tue-Sun 1000-1700; mid-Sep to mid-May Tue-Sun 1100-1700. ISK 1000, concessions ISK 500. Free entry with Reykjavík Welcome Card. Café Tue-Sun 1100-1630.

The National Gallery has a vast collection of art but the lack of space means only a limited amount of pieces can be displayed. This building displays work from the most significant Icelandic artists – including Ásgrímur Jónsson – as well as up-and-coming artists and a large Danish collection. The focus is largely on 19th- and 20th-century artists but the museum's collection also includes work from internationally renowned artists including Munch and Picasso. Exhibitions are held over three floors and there is also a lovely café with a view of the pond and a decent Icelandic art book shop. The building itself was constructed as a freezing plant in 1920 and later became one of Reykjavík's most popular dance clubs before it burnt down in 1971. In 1988 it was restored and became the nation's art gallery.

Old Graveyard

Across the pond, on Suðurgata, just off Tjarnargata, the old graveyard is worth a wander round to give you an insight into the unusual patronymic naming system. You'll see a number of Viking-style memorials here, too, and there's a poetic,

1 Reykjavík

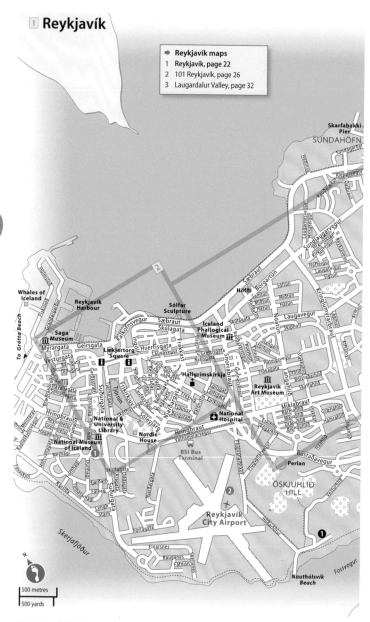

Skarfabakki Pier
SUNDAHÖFN

Whales of Iceland

Reykjavík Harbour

Sólfar Sculpture

Höfði

To Grótta Beach

Saga Museum

Iceland Phallogical Museum

Lækjartorg Square

Hallgrímskirkja

Reykjavík Art Museum

National & University Library

National Hospital

Nordic House

National Museum of Iceland

BSÍ Bus Terminal

Perlan

ÖSKJUHLÍÐ HILL

Reykjavík City Airport

Skerjafjörður

Nauthólsvík Beach

Fossvogur

N

500 metres
500 yards

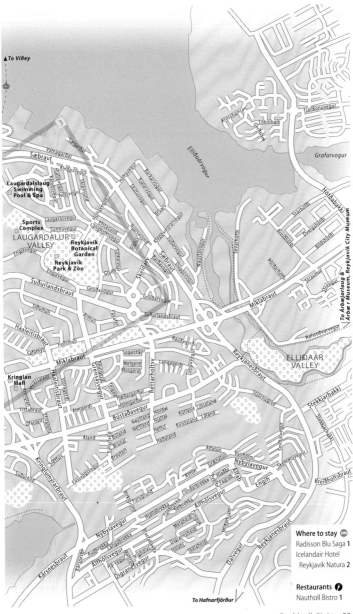

Where to stay 🛏
Radisson Blu Saga **1**
Icelandair Hotel
Reykjavik Natura **2**

Restaurants 🍴
Nautholl Bistro **1**

bohemian atmosphere about the place. Look out for the memorial to the father of the republic, Jón Sigurdsson, and Magnus Magnússon's grave. It's not the final resting place of the father of Mastermind though, and just goes to show that with a patronymic naming system such as this (see Language, page 110, for details), it's not surprising that there are a few namesakes in this country!

★National Museum of Iceland
Suðurgata 41, T530 2200, www.nationalmuseum.is. 1 May-15 Sep daily 1000-1700; 16 Sep-30 Apr Tue-Sun 1100-1700. ISK 1500, senior citizens and students ISK 750, children free. Free with Reykjavik Welcome Card. Shop and café.

The National Museum takes you through 1200 years of Iceland's history, displaying the country's stunning Viking past with graves, carvings and writing through the time of settlement to the present day. The museum's permanent exhibition 'The making of a nation' is conceived as a journey through time, beginning on a boat in which the medieval settlers crossed the ocean to their new home, and ending with an airport, the modern Icelanders' gateway to the world. The displays cover diverse aspects of the country's history and culture, including multimedia displays on topics such as mythology, the construction of early Viking buildings, the adoption of Christianity, the Reformation and the Census of 1703. Downstairs, temporary photographic exhibitions tell tales of life in Reykjavík today, while in the shop you can buy anything from a knitted Icelandic beard cap to ancient Icelandic-style children's toys made from whale bones. There is a small café serving snacks and coffee.

Nordic House (Norræna Húsið)
Sturlugata 5, T551 7030, www.nordichouse.is. Exhibitions Tue-Sun 1200-1700, ISK 300. Library daily 1200-1700, free.

This building represents something of a cultural link between Iceland and other Nordic countries, with a library of modern Scandinavian literature, a café and an exhibition hall. The building was designed by contemporary Finnish architect, Alvar Aalto, and is very modern and unusual in design. Classical concerts are often held here, as are occasional Scandinavian-themed events and some edgy and inspiring exhibitions, which have recently concerned themselves with street art and Nordic photography. The biggest draw, however, is its restaurant **Dill**, hailed as the best in the city, which serves what else but New Nordic cuisine.

Bankastræti and Skolavörðustígur
These streets, to the east of Austurvöllur Square and south of Lækjartorg Square, are characterized by a colourful array of corrugated-iron-clad houses and shops dating from around 1910-1930. **Bankastræti** is one of the best places to begin your bar crawl in the evening, or alternatively somewhere to rest up in a café after a walk round town. As you continue along it, it becomes **Laugavegur**, the main shopping street in the city, which runs a few kilometers along to Laugardalur Valley. There are a number of good restaurants in this area to suit all budgets. The

streets here are ideal for souvenir hunting, especially **Skólavörðustigur** with its small independent art galleries and craft shops.

Hallgrímskirkja
Skólavörðustigur, T510 1000, www.hallgrimskirkja.is. Daily 0900-1700. Tower view ISK 800, children ISK 100.

Reykjavík's answer to the Eiffel Tower stands at the top of Skólavörðustígur and offers views of the city to as far as the Snæfellsnes Peninsula on a clear day. Reminiscent of a volcanic eruption, the building was designed by state architect Guðjón Samúelson following a national competition to create a church for the hilltop to hold 1200 people with a 74-m-high tower that could double as a radio mast. Some 49 years in the making (1945-1986), it's as impressive inside as out and the steeple has the best view of the city by far. The church is named after the Reverend Hallgrímur Pétursson (1614-1675), the country's foremost hymn writer, whose hymns are still regularly sung today. Three co-ordinated bells in the tower are named after him, his wife Guðríður and his daughter Steinunn. The church holds services at 1100 on Sundays for its 7000 parishioners. It also holds occasional classical concerts.

Einar Jónsson Museum
Eiriksgata T551 3797, www.lej.is. 1 Jun-15 Sep Tue-Sun 1300-1700, closed Mon; 16 Sep-31 May Sat-Sun 1300-1700, closed weekdays; closed Dec-Jan. ISK 1000, concessions (students and senior citizens) ISK 500; under 18s free. Garden open year round, free.

Einar Jónsson (1874-1954), Iceland's first sculptor, studied in Denmark and was a groundbreaking abstract sculptor. This museum stands adjacent to Hallgrímskirkja, where he chose to locate it, in his own words, on "a desolate hill on the outskirts of town". Originally intended to be more of a cultural centre, it's certainly a nexus for tourist traffic with the imposing church so close. The museum is well worth a look if you like allegorical and classical sculpture; the garden is a nice place to relax on a sunny day amid the bronzes.

Kjarvalsstaðir (Reykjavík Art Museum)
Flókagata, 105 Reykjavík, T517 1290, www.listasafnreykjavikur.is. Daily 1000-1700. ISK 1400, students ISK 800, concessions and under 18s free. Free with Reykjavík Welcome Card.

Not technically in 101 but a short walk from it, this has the best range of Icelandic and foreign art. Don't be disappointed by the exterior of this gallery which seems a little concrete and uninspiring, inside is a welcoming and open space with contemporary international and Icelandic photography and artwork. Kjarvalsstaðir is named after the romantic and bohemian Icelandic artist Jóhannes S Kjarval (1885-1972) who donated many of his works and belongings to the city in 1968. Exhibitions from the Kjarval collection are regularly on display here; abstract renderings of Icelandic landscapes complete with personifications of the

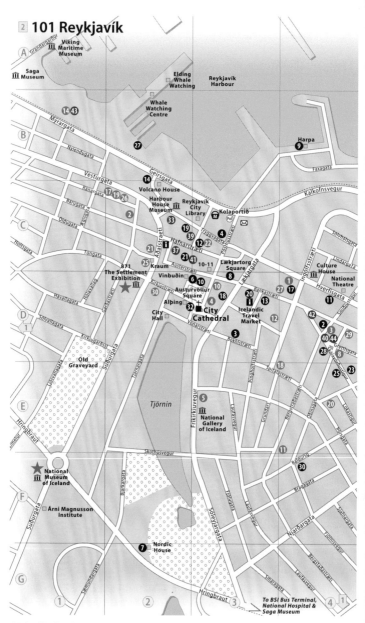

Viking Maritime Museum

Saga Museum

Elding Whale Watching

Reykjavík Harbour

Whale Watching Centre

Harpa

Mýrargata

Nýlendugata

Vesturgata

Geirsgata

Faxagata

Kalkofnsvegur

Volcano House

Harbour House Museum

Reykjavík City Library

Kolaportið

Sólvholtsgata

Ránargata

Bárugata

Öldugata

Vesturgata

Hafnarstræti

Tryggvagata

Lindargata

Culture House

National Theatre

Holtsgata

Tungata

Aðalstræti

Austurstræti

10-11

Lækjartorg Square

Ingólfsstræti

Bankastræti

Hverfisgata

871 The Settlement Exhibition

Kraum

Vínbúðin

Austurvöllur Square

Alþingi

City Hall

City Cathedral

Icelandic Travel Market

Bókhlöðustígur

Hafnarstræti

Laugavegur

Klapparstígur

Grettisgata

Havallagata

Kirkjustræti

Vonarstræti

Sólvallagata

Hringbraut

Tjörnin

Frikirkjuvegur

National Gallery of Iceland

Laufásvegur

Þingholtsstræti

Bergstaðastræti

Skálholtsstígur

Grundarstígur

Óðinsgata

Baldursgata

Spítalastígur

Freyjugata

Skothúsvegur

Bragagata

Bjargargata

National Museum of Iceland

Árni Magnusson Institute

Old Graveyard

Suðurgata

Tjarnargata

Laufásvegur

Njarðargata

Nordic House

Hringbraut

Smáragata

Sóleyjargata

Fjólugata

Njálsgata

To BSÍ Bus Terminal, National Hospital & Saga Museum

N

200 metres
200 yards

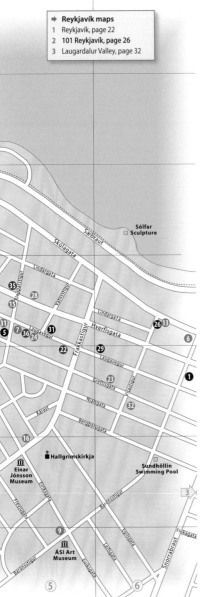

Sólfar
☐ Sculpture

Skúlagata

Lindargata

Sæbraut

Hverfisgata

Laugavegur

Grettisgata

Njálsgata

Bergþórugata

Kárastígur

⛪ Hallgrímskirkja

🏛 Einar Jónsson Museum

Sundhöllin Swimming Pool

3

🏛 ÁSÍ Art Museum

Snorrabraut

Flókagata

Eiríksgata

Þórsgata

Freyjugata

Njarðargata

Where to stay 🛏
101 **1** *D4*
Apotek **10** *D3*
Alfholl Guesthouse **2** *C2*
Apartment K **3** *D4*
Borg **4** *D3*
Castle House
  Apartment & Embassy
  Luxury Apartments **5** *E3*
Fosshotel Baron **6** *D6*
Frón **7** *D5*
Guesthouse Adam **8** *D4*
Guesthouse Sunna **9** *G5*
Holt **11** *E4*
Home **12** *D3*
Hostel Kex **13** *D6*
Icelandair Reykjavik
  Marina **14** *B1*
Klopp **15** *D5*
Leifur Eiriksson **16** *F5*
Lighthouse
  Apartments **17** *C2*
Luna Apartments **18** *E4*
Metropolitan **19** *C2*
Odinsve **20** *E4*
Plaza **21** *C2*
Radisson Blu 1919 **22** *C3*
Rey Apartments **23** *E6*
Reykjavik Backpackers
  24 *D5*
Reykjavik Centrum **25** *C2*
Reykjavik Downtown
  Hostel **26** *C2*
Reykjavik Loft Hostel
  27 *D4*
Reykjavik Residence
  28 *D5*
Room with a view **29** *D4*
Salvation Army
  Guest House **30** *D2*
Skjaldbreid **31** *D5*
Tower Guesthouse **32** *E6*

Restaurants 🍴
Argentina **1** *E6*
Asia **2** *D4*
B5 **3** *D3*
Baejarins Beztu **4** *C3*
Café Gardurinn **5** *D5*
Café Paris **6** *D3*
Dill **7** *G2*
Einar Ben **8** *D3*
Gandhi **10** *D3*
Grai Kotturinn **11** *D4*
Hornid **12** *C3*
Humarhusid **13** *D3*
Icelandic Fish n chips
  14 *B2*
Islenskibarinn **17** *D4*
Jomfruin **18** *D3*
Krua Thai **19** *C2*
Laekjarbrekka **20** *D3*
The Laundromat Café
  21 *C2*
Mokka Café **23** *E4*
Noodle Station **25** *E4*
Saemundur
  at Hostel Kex **26** *D6*
Sea Baron **27** *B2*
Sjarvargrillid **28** *D4*
Smurstodin **9** *B4*
Te og Kaffe **29** *E6*
Thrir Frakkar **30** *F4*
Tiu Dropar **31** *D5*
Vid Tjornina **32** *D2*

Bars & clubs 🍸
Bakkhus **33** *C2*
Café Rosenberg **35** *D5*
Dillon Whiskey Bar **36** *D5*
Dolly **37** *C2*
Harlem **39** *D4*
Kaffibarinn **40** *D4*
The Lebowski Bar **22** *E5*
Microbar **41** *C3*
Prikid **42** *D4*
Slippbarinn **43** *B1*
Vegamot **44** *D4*

Reykjavík Sights•27

elements. Kjarval particularly enjoyed characterizing the way that colour changes in response to varying light, a particularly Icelandic characteristic of nature.

Culture House (Safnahúsið)
Hverfisgata 15, T545 1400, www.thjodmenning.is. Daily 1100-1700. ISK 1500, senior citizens and students ISK 750, children free. Free with Reykjavik Welcome Card.

The large white Culture House (formerly the city library) is a unique venue promoting Iceland's cultural heritage and art history. Recently reopened after a substantial redevelopment, the innovative new exhibition 'Points of view' brings together collections from six of the country's major cultural institutions, from 4000-year-old artefacts to the latest in Icelandic art. Covering four floors, the displays aim to shed light on the way visual art has been used throughout history to express ideas about the world, our environment and ourselves and to show how the materials and techniques have changed. Visitors are encouraged to make connections between old and new, for example, a medieval manuscript and a modern painting, and to reflect on the importance of the nation's visual legacy.

Harpa
Austurbakki 2, T528 5000, www.harpa.is. Daily 0800-2400 (depending on events). Free. 45-min guided tours Mon-Fri 1530, Sat-Sun 1100 and 1530, ISK 1750.

This modern fish-scaled building beside the old harbour is Reykjavík's architectural showpiece. Designed in part by Icelandic-Danish artist Olafur Eliasson, it has extensive conference facilities as well as concert halls, restaurants, a music shop and a design store. The design was based on crystallized basalt columns and is kaleidoscopic and dazzling, particularly from the inside. Look out for big name artists playing here – one of the ideas behind the centre was that it would allow access to European and North American musicians, of every persuasion, as well as Icelandic artists, and it has hosted everyone from Jamie Cullum to Yoko Ono and Björk. Next door, a new hotel is being planned primarily for business and conference purposes to open around 2016.

Museum of Photography (Ljósmyndasafn)
6th floor, Grófarhús, Tryggvagata 15, T411 6300, www.ljosmyndasafnreykjavikur.is/en. Exhibitions Mon-Thu 1200-1900, Fri 1200-1800, Sat-sun 1300-1700. Free.

On the top floor of the city library, this free exhibition is worth a look for its interesting permanent and temporary displays. With an archive of five million photos dating from 1870 to 2002, the exhibits present a cross-section of artistic, social and cultural aspects of Iceland society from industrial landscapes to family portraits and press photography.

Harbour House Museum (Harfnarhús)
Tryggvagata 17, T590 1211, www.listasafnreykjavikur.is. Fri-Wed 1000-1700, Thu 1000-2000. ISK 1400, students ISK 800, concessions and under 18s free. Free with Reykjavík Welcome Card.

Part of the Reykjavík Art Museum, Harbour House shows diverse exhibitions of work by Icelandic and foreign artists with a focus on modern art and installations. There is a permanent exhibition by contemporary Icelandic artist Erró, famed for his post-surrealist paintings, Peter Blake–style collages and narrative paintings, many of which he donated to the city of Reykjavík in 1989. They're a lot of fun and politically charged at the same time. Look out particularly for his 'pope art' amid the pop art. The gallery also has a café with a pleasant view of the harbour, and a small shop.

Kolaportið Flea Market
Tryggvagata 19, T562 5030, www.kolaportid.is. Sat-Sun 1100-1700. Free.

Iceland's biggest flea market is held each weekend in the old customs building by the quay. Here' you will find a host of stalls selling everything from bric-a-brac and second-hand clothing to a wide range of Icelandic books and handmade Lopis. If you're looking for an Icelandic jumper but baulk at the prices in the tourist shops, come here – they are much better value. There is also a good and cheap fish market where you can try some of the country's more dubious culinary delights, including rotten shark and dried fish.

Víking Maritime Museum
Grandagarði 8, T411 6300, www.maritimemuseum.is. Daily 1000-1700; guided tours of the Óðinn daily at 1300, 1400, 1500. Museum ISK 1400; tour of the Óðinn ISK 1200; museum and tour ISK 2000; students ISK 800, concessions and under 18s free. Shop and café. Free with Reykjavik Welcome Card.

Situated in an old fish factory with a great view over the harbour, this museum celebrates Reykjavík's age-old relationship with the sea. As a fishing and international shipping port, the entire Icelandic economy was long based upon the fisheries, and even today the ocean and its resources play a key role in Icelandic life. The museum focuses on maritime history and the fisheries over the centuries, presenting information through exhibits and models, as well as state-of-the-art video and computer technology. You can also visit the coast guard vessel *Odinn*, which participated in all the three cod wars waged against Britain in the latter half of the 20th century. There's also a shop, café and children's play area. It's good family fun.

Whales of Iceland
Fiskislóð 23, T571 0077, www.whalesoficeland.is/en. May-Sep daily 0900-1900, Oct-Apr daily 0900-1800. ISK 2900, children (7-15 years) ISK 1500, under 7s free.

Reykjavík's latest harbourside venture is Europe's largest whale museum. The huge state-of-the-art exhibition space has impressive life-sized models suspended from the ceiling of all the different types of whales known to inhabit Icelandic waters. Ambient whale sounds and blue lighting make for a tranquil learning experience as you wander beneath the enormous cetaceans exploring the interactive displays. The museum aims to encourage respect for whales and their habitat and to explore the sad impact of humans on these magnificent creatures. It's an interesting place to explore, especially before or after seeing the huge mammals in real life on a whale-watching trip.

Saga Museum
Grandagardi 2, T511 1517, www.sagamuseum.is. Daily 1000-1800. ISK 2000, concessions ISK 1500, children ISK 800. Café and shop.

Recently expanded after moving to new harbourside premises, this is one of Iceland's best Viking museums, charting the early history of the country through the stories of the sagas. It's colourful, bloodthirsty and full of feuding Vikings, not to mention witches burned at the stake, and offers a real insight into Iceland's history and literature. Great for kids.

Viðey Island
3 km offshore, T533 5055, www.videy.com. The Viðey Island ferry runs several times daily from Skarfabakki Pier (Oct to mid-May weekends only), return ticket ISK 1100, children (7-15s) ISK 550, under 6s free. Free with Reykjavik Welcome Card.

It takes just a few minutes by ferry to reach the small, historical island of Viðey and is a particularly fun day trip for families. The island was inhabited as early as the 10th century and the oldest stone building in Iceland was discovered there. The monastery, found during excavations, dates from the 13th century when it was the richest in the country. Following the Reformation in the 16th century, the island passed to the secular lords, then became a fishing community and is now inhabited by hundreds of birds that enjoy the rich grassland. There's a restaurant and a church and some lovely walks plus Icelandic pony riding opportunities in the summer months.

Inside the old schoolhouse on the island you'll find a photographic exhibition about Viðey and there's also a coffee house selling hot chocolate and snacks. Guided walks are offered in the summer and around the cliffs you'll see many thousands of seabirds. You can also see the nearby island of **Lundey**, home to tens of thousands of puffins.

Perhaps the most notable sight on the island is Yoko Ono's **Imagine Peace Tower**. She conceived this work of art as a beacon to world peace. It is dedicated to the memory of John Lennon and sends up a beam of light visible every day after sunset from 9 October (John Lennon's birthday) and 8 December (the date of his death). It is also lit for the winter solstice for a week, New Year's Eve and on the spring equinox. There are also some other artworks on the island including carved basalt columns by US sculptor Richard Serra and inscribed stones by unknown artists.

Harbour walks and Sólfar sculpture
Walking east along the harbour on a clear day gives you fine views of Viðey Island with Mount Esja looming over it and the delicate scent of fish in the air. It's a very enjoyable 10-minute walk up to the Viking boat sculpture, but it can be windy

and a little exposed. The sculpture itself, *Sólfar*, meaning 'Sun Voyager' points out towards sea and was made by Jón Gunnar Árnarson in 1971. It looks like it's floating on water itself, mounted on polished marble and gleaming silver against the sky.

Look across the main Sæbraut road back towards the city and you'll see **Höfði**, a cream-coloured wooden clapboard building. It's the reception house of the city council and hosted the momentous summit meeting of Reagan and Gorbachev in October 1986 which led to the end of the Cold War.

Walk in the other direction, or preferably take a bike, and you can reach the lighthouse on the edge of the Seltjarnes Peninsula and lonely **Grótta Beach**. The walk takes about two to three hours and runs right along the harbour's edge; bus 3 also runs in this direction. Alternatively, walk the length of Vesturgata and when you reach the sea follow the path along the shore to the end. Grótta Beach itself is unspoilt, unlike Nauthólsvík Beach, and you can sit and watch the seabirds.

Laugardalur Valley
scenic area for walking, climbing and thermal swimming pools

The name Reykjavík literally translates as 'smoky bay', as the first settlers mistook the steam from the hot springs in the Laugardalur Valley for smoke. This is the city's most important sports area, containing the National Indoor Stadium and football pitch as well as an Olympic-sized swimming pool and luxury spa complex. The springs are still used today in the comfortably warm pool and its various hot pots, and they're well worth a visit.

Icelandic Phallological Museum
Laugavegur 116, 101 Reykjavík, T561 6663, www.phallus.is. May-Sep daily 1000-1800; Oct-Apr 1100-1800. ISK 1250; concessions ISK 1000; children under 13 free.

Possibly the only museum in the world dedicated to the penis, the Icelandic Phallological Museum boasts a collection of all the penises you could find from all the types of mammal in Iceland. There are almost 60 specimens, including those from 17 types of whale, one polar bear, seven types of seal and walrus and plenty of land mammals too, yes, even humans. There are also a good few novelty items like penis-shaped telephones and bull's testicle lampshades to snigger at.

Laugardalslaug Thermal Pool and Spa
Sundlaugavegur 104, 105 Reykjavík, T411 5100. Mon-Fri 0630-2200, Sat-Sun 0800-2200. ISK 650, children ISK 140. Free with Reykjavík Welcome Card. Towel rental from ISK 550. Massages from ISK 4500 for 30 mins, www.lauganudd.is. Bus 14 from Lækjartorg Sq.

This is the biggest of the city's seven thermal pools, attracting tourists and residents alike for the 50-m-pool, slide, hot pots, steam room and sauna. Note that Icelandic swimming pool etiquette requires you to wash thoroughly without a swimming costume before entering the pool, and attendants see that you do.

It's a real chance to see what Icelanders do – going to the swimming pool has the same cultural weight in Iceland as going to the pub in the UK. Note too that these swimming pools are a snip compared to swimming at the Blue Lagoon – and you're also swimming in geothermal water in the open air here. You can book a massage at the same pool and there is a gym next door too.

Ásmunder Sveinsson Sculpture Museum (Ásmundarsafn)

Sigtún, 105 Reykjavík, T553 2155, www.listasafnreykjavikur.is. May-Sep daily 1000-1700, Oct-Apr 1300-1700. ISK 1400, students ISK 800, concessions and under 18s free. Free with Reykjavík Welcome Card. Bus 14 from Lækjartorg Sq.

Across the road from the sports complex you'll see an unusual white domed building surrounded by sculptures. It could almost be a space observatory, but is actually the former home and now museum of Ásmunder Sveinsson, one of the pioneers of Icelandic sculpture. Thirty of his abstract Henry Moore-like sculptures

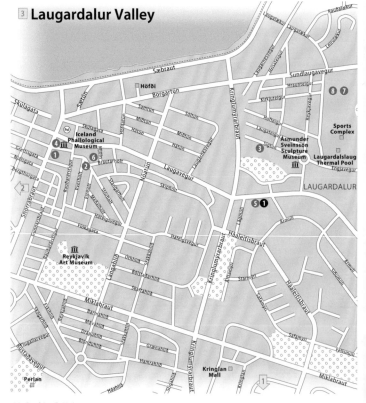

③ **Laugardalur Valley**

are displayed outside the building for free all year round, while inside the more delicate works are displayed, many of which draw on Icelandic literature, fairytales and nature. It's well worth a visit.

Reykjavík Park and Zoo
Hafrafell v/ Engjaveg, 105 Reykjavík, T575 7800, www.mu.is. Daily 1000-1700. ISK 750, children (5-12s) ISK 550, under 4s free. Free with Reykjavik Welcome Card. Buses 2, 10, 11, 12 or 15 from Lækjartorg Sq.

Behind the sports complex and next to the botanical garden, the park and zoo is great for families, with farm animals, seals, mink, reindeer and a small petting zoo. It's ideal for toddlers up to age eight. There's also a playground, small train, mini-fairground, pond with boats and a small snackbar/café. Families with small children could happily spend a morning or afternoon here, with a walk around the botanical garden next door to burn off energy too.

➡ Reykjavík maps
1 Reykjavík, page 22
2 101 Reykjavík, page 26
3 **Laugardalur Valley, page 32**

Where to stay 🛏
4th Floor 1
Einholt Apartments 2
Grand Hotel Reykjavik 3
Guesthouse 101 4
Hilton Nordica 5
Klettur 6
Reykjavik Campsite 7
Reykjavik City Hostel 8

Restaurants 🍴
Vox 1

Reykjavík Botanical Garden
Laugardalur, 105 Reykjavík, T411 8650, www.grasagardur.is. May-Sep daily 1000-2200, Oct-Apr 1000-1500. Café Flora May-Sep. Free. Buses 2, 10, 11, 12, 15.

The botanical garden is a joy on a clear sunny day, with 2.5 ha of good walking and cycling trails along the rock gardens, Japanese-style bridges, and Icelandic flora, such as it is. There's a small hothouse and café too. It's Reykjavík's answer to Central Park, though obviously on a much smaller scale, and is unusual in that it's one of the most wooded parts of the capital. There's an arboretum and a woodland area and this is one of the few places where the joke "What should you do if you get lost in an Icelandic forest? Stand up!" doesn't work. You can also see where the original hot springs were, where women used to cook, clean and make a kind of whey cheese, and the park is overlooked by the **Áskirkja**, a basalt church which looks like a ship's prow. The camping ground and youth hostel back onto the park.

Öskjuhlíð Hill

Dominated by the Pearl, Öskjuhlíð Hill was used by the British Army in the Second World War and has a number of walking and cycling trails around the hillside and down to the beach. Between the Pearl and the sea there's an artificial geyser which goes off roughly every five minutes and gives an idea of what lies in store at Geysir. The trees and shrubs could be said to constitute an Icelandic forest and it's worth exploring on foot, bike or rollerblades.

The Pearl (Perlan)

Öskjuhlíð Hill, 105 Reykjavík, T562 0200, www.perlan.is. Observatory daily 1000-2330. Free. Café 1130-2200. Bus 13 from Lækjartorg Sq.

Built atop the city's hot-water storage tanks, Perlan is an amazing modern glass building with wonderful views across the city and out to sea. It became one of the city's iconic buildings when it opened in 1991 and art exhibitions, expos and concerts are regularly held here. The fourth floor has a small café with particularly good ice creams and a viewing deck. From here you can see out to the president's home of Bessastaðir as well as a volcanic ridge and the city airport. The fifth floor has an exceptional restaurant with a revolving floor that takes two hours to make a full circuit of the city and there's also a bar on the sixth floor.

Nauthólsvík Beach

Follow the woodland trail down to the Ægisíða shore for about 7 mins and you'll find the man-made and very quirky Nauthólsvík Beach. Buses 3, 4 and 6 go to Ægisíða, and bus 5 goes to Skeljarnes for a shorter walk. Alternatively, take bus 7 to Perlan and walk down the hill. Daily 15 May-15 Aug 1000-1900; 16 Aug-14 May Mon-Fri 1100-1300, Sat 1100-1500. Free in summer; ISK 500 in winter. Towel rental ISK 300.

Not only have they imported yellow sand here, as opposed to the naturally occurring black volcanic stuff, but there's a hot tub on the beach and the sea is pumped with geothermal water to keep it at 18-20°C. Icelanders even swim here in the winter when it's not heated at all – think of it as one of those strange Scandinavian quirks. If it's a nice day be warned: the beach is quite small and you might find yourself fighting for that last patch of man-made sand. Note that the lagoon is only heated during opening hours and that there is a small charge (ISK 200) for storing clothes in lockers. There are changing rooms and a small, cheap café right on the beach as well as the lovely turf-roofed **Nauthóll Bistro** a short walk away.

Elliðaár Valley

The Elliðaár Valley, a 20-minute drive east of Reykjavík, is a lush green valley with a salmon river running through it, a thermal swimming pool, **Reykjavík Art Museum** (**Kjarvalsstadir**) and, apparently, quite a few elves. There are a couple of historic sites here including **Þingnes**, south of the lake, thought to be one of the oldest places of assembly in Iceland. The fishing season runs from 15 June to

14 September. There are also a number of good hiking and biking trails in the area and some pony trekking tours head out this way. Contact the tourist information centre for further details.

Árbær Museum (Árbæjarsafn)

Kistuhyl 4, 110 Reykjavík, T411 6300, www.minjasafnreykjavikur.is. Jun-Aug daily 1000-1700, otherwise by arrangement. Guided tours daily at 1300 in summer. ISK 1400, concessions and under 18s free. Free with Reykjavik Welcome Card. Bus 110 from Lækjartorg Sq or bus 10 from Hlemmur.

Árbæjarsafn is an open-air museum tracing the architecture and history of Reykjavík. Most of the houses originally come from the city centre with the oldest dating back to 1820. It's certainly an interesting peek into the past, showing clearly how the city has grown in the last 50 years, before which it was an oddment of houses scattered around the pond. Local actors dress up as workers from days gone by and there is an interesting collection of toys from the past. There's also a café in the midst of all the turf-roofed houses and it's a pleasant place to spend a sunny afternoon.

About a 15- to 20-minute walk from the museum along the river is the **Árbæjarlaug** outdoor swimming pool. It has a fantastic view and feels as though it's right in the countryside.

Hafnarfjörður
surrounded by lava fields and more elves than Tolkien would know what to do with

Known as 'the town in the lava', Hafnarfjörður (pronounced Hab-nar-fyur-thur) is the most interesting of the city's suburbs. It's only 10 km from the centre of Reykjavík and easy to reach by bus and car. The town encircles the harbour, with lava fields around it, and is a nice walking area. While you're there, look out for the elves, or 'hidden people' – *huldufólk* – who, legend has it, live in the lava.

Hafnarfjörður is said to have the highest population of other-worldly beings of any town in Iceland. This may be tourist hype, too much *brennivín* or a trick of the light, you can decide for yourself.

Hafnarfjörður is on Route 1 towards Keflavík. Bus S1 runs every 20 minutes from Lækjartorg Square. It's a family-friendly suburb, but eating and drinking doesn't compare to the city and the 10-minute drive into Reykjavík is certainly worth it for the restaurants and nightlife.

The **tourist information centre** ① *Town Hall, Strandgata 6, 220 Reykjavík, T585 5500, www.hafnarfjordur.is, Mon-Fri 0800-1600*, is very helpful and friendly and can provide details of six themed walks of the town and a *Hidden Worlds* map, as well as booking accommodation and tours. There is an additional tourist office at the Hafnarfjörður Museum, Vesturgata 8 (see page 38), which is open June-August daily 1100-1700; otherwise weekends only 1100-1700. The website www.visithafnarfjordur.is is useful for information.

Hafnarfjörður

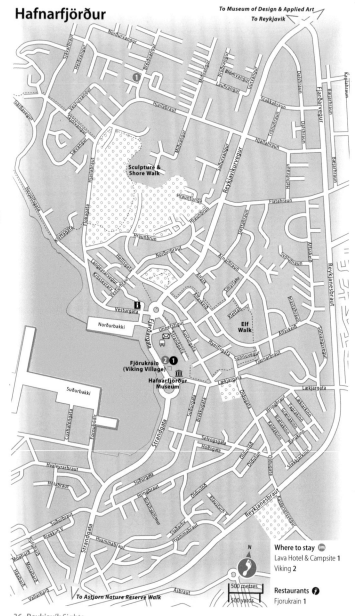

To Museum of Design & Applied Art

To Reykjavik

Sculpture & Shore Walk

Elf Walk

Fjörukráin (Viking Village)

Hafnarfjörður Museum

Norðurbakki

Suðurbakki

To Astjorn Nature Reserve Walk

Where to stay 🛌
Lava Hotel & Campsite **1**
Viking **2**

Restaurants 🍴
Fjorukrain **1**

N

500 metres
500 yards

Away with the fairies

Myths and legends surround Iceland and those about the 'hidden people' or *huldufólk* are among the most delightful. Up to a quarter of the population are said to have some kind of belief in elves, and there was even, until recently, an elf school in Reykjavík seeking to educate people about the 13 types of hidden people living in Iceland, and keeping the fairy tales alive.

Elf watching, elf spotting and talking about the hidden people are traditions that are particularly alive in the Reykjavík suburb of Hafnarfjörður where a local seer has drawn a map depicting the best of the town's other-worldly dwellings. It's said that one of the roads into the town is routed around a large rock because it is a home for hidden people, and that every time the builders tried to knock it down, the hidden people broke their machinery until they had no choice but to route around it. Centuries old folktales also say that the clans of Iceland's hidden people live in the rocks in the centre of the town.

There are many different kind of beings to be found in the gardens of the town, a town surrounded by lava which is particularly popular with them. There are the classic *álfar* – elves – who can be of many different sizes and shapes: the *huldufólk*, or 'hidden people', who look very much like humans, live together in social groups and supposedly move things in your house; the *ljúflingar*, 'lovelings', slender and graceful beings the size of 10-year-olds; temperamental *dvergar*, 'dwarves', about the size of toddlers; and the amazing *tívar*, 'mountain spirits'. You'd certainly know if you saw one of these creatures, beautiful, bright and several hundred metres tall with a warmth radiating from them. You have to have second sight to be able to see them, of course.

Visitors to Hafnarfjörður can go on guided tours with an experienced seer, taking place on Tuesdays and Fridays in the summer, and by arrangement at other times. Visit www.alfar.is for details. There is also a Hidden Worlds iPhone tour of Hafnarfjörður with commentary – contact the tourist information centre (see page 39) for more information. The town also has a small lava park called the **Elf's Garden** with an information centre and café serving elf-related drinks: www.elfgarden.is.

Other parts of Iceland have their own elf traditions and you might see the odd house painted on rocks as you drive around the south, to remind humans of the *huldufólk*. Icelanders have a particularly close bond with nature and their environment, not least because its drama invades on their lives on a regular basis in the shape of volcanoes, earthquakes and weather extremes, as well as to their ancestors, so perhaps their beliefs stem from these unusual circumstances. Traditional Icelandic folk tales have underlying themes of keeping in harmony with nature and strong moral values, traditions that serve a great purpose in a country of such extraordinary scenery.

Walks around town

There are a number of scenic routes to take around the town, the cliffs and the lava. The **Sculpture and Shore Walk** starts from the tourist office on Vesturgata. Walk up the road away from the harbour and down Herjólfsgata and along the coast. The **Elf Walk** begins where Hellisgata and Reykjavíkurvegur meet. Walk to the Hellisgerði park which has a bonsai garden and is home to a colony of elves. Then head back down Reykjavíkurvegur and take a left down Hverfisgata. Some more elves live on the left-hand side of the road. Another good place to check out is to the top of Hellisgerði park at Nönnustígur where a several-hundred-year-old hermit lives. He's reputed to be friendly and relaxed.

The **Ástjörn Nature Reserve**, around the lake in the south of Hafnarfjörður, is a pleasant walk. Ásfjall is the smallest mountain in Iceland and is a good viewpoint over the harbour and surrounding area as well as into the lava and away to Helgafell in the other direction.

Viking Village (Fjörukráin)
Strandgata 55, T565 1213, www.fjorukrain.is. Daily 1200-2200.

Along the harbour from the tourist information centre you can see a strange looking wooden building with a carved dragon at its peak. This is the Fjörukráin Viking Village, a replica Viking hall and hotel serving up traditional feasts. The food, including lamb, schnapps and *skyr*, a thick yoghurty dessert, is exceptional and a banquet of traditional fare costs ISK 8900 including drinks and some great Viking and Valkyrie impersonations. You can also drink in their Viking cave and be part of a staged group kidnapping. As well as feasts from 1800 daily, the village also has 14 Viking houses decorated in Viking style for visitors and a Viking hotel. Contact them directly for bookings, see page 44.

Hafnarfjörður Museum
Various locations, www.hafnarfjordur.is/museum.

Hafnarfjörður Museum is housed in a number of buildings and outposts around the town. The main building, **Pakkhúsið** ⓘ *Vesturgata 6, Jun-Aug daily 1100-1700,* is a renovated 19th-century warehouse and consists of a children's toys exhibition, a historical museum containing a number of texts, photographs and artefacts about Hafnarfjörður and a photographic exhibition. There is a small tourist office here in summer (see page 35).

The museum also has two other houses on display: **Sívertsen House** ⓘ *Vesturgata 6, Jun-Aug daily 1100-1700,* is the oldest house in Hafnarfjörður and has been restored to its original state. It's a good example of an upper-class home in the early 19th century. By contrast, **Sigga's House** ⓘ *Kirkjuvegur 10, Jun-Aug Sat-Sun 1100-1700,* is an example of a working-class home in the early 20th century.

Museum of Design and Applied Art
Garðatorg, 210 Garðabær, T512 1525, www.honnunarsafn.is. Jun-Aug Sat-Sun 1100-1700.

This museum is 8 km from Reykjavík between Hafnarfjörður and the city and focuses on modern Icelandic design from 1900 to the present day. It has regular exhibitions and events as well as a small shop. Worth a visit if you're interested in Scandinavian design – it's the only place in the country that really examines it properly.

Listings Reykjavík *maps p22, p26, p32, p36*

Tourist information

Visit Reykjavik
Aðalstræti 2, 101 Reykjavik, T590 1550, www.visitreykjavik.is. Daily 1 Jun-15 Sep 0830-1900, 16 Sep-31 May Mon-Fri 0900-1800, Sat 0900-1600, Sun 0900-1400.
A great first stop for advice, excursion booking services, maps and weather forecasting. They also have internet access. There is a small concession in Keflavik Airport. For information on the **Reykjavík Welcome Card**, see page 18.

Icelandic Travel Market (ITM)
Bankastræti 2, T522 4979, www.icelandictravelmarket.is. Daily Jun-Aug 0800-2100; rest of the year 0900-1900.
Just off the main shopping street, ITM offers tourist information and booking services.

Where to stay

The densest concentration of hotels, hostels, B&Bs and apartments is in the central 101 or old town district, and it's certainly the best place to stay. Boutique hotels, designer apartments and fantastic hostels are the pick of the bunch; book ahead for the best bargains or even better, spend some time trawling travel websites for deals and offers. If you're visiting in high season (Jun-Aug) expect to spend a little more for the privilege. Families or groups visiting should certainly consider apartment rental or apartment hotels – there are plenty in the city at every price and style point.

101 Reykjavík

€€€€ Apotek Hotel
Austurstraeti 16, T512 9000, www.keahotels.is/apotek-hotel.
Reykjavík's newest boutique hotel has a prestigious location in a historic building and landmark, formerly the central pharmacy. The interior is modern and smart with 45 rooms and suites, a restaurant and bar, spread out over 6 floors.

€€€€ Hotel 101
Hverfisgata 10, T580 0101, www.101hotel.is.
Opposite the Culture House and the National Opera, this new and ultra-fashionable boutique outfit has sculptures, murals, Icelandic art and an airy bar and restaurant. It's all very minimalist chic with lots of reflective surfaces, huge showers and freestanding baths. The spa and gym downstairs will help you keep as glam as the surroundings.

€€€€ Hotel Borg
Pósthússtræti 11, T551 1440, www.hotelborg.is.

Reykjavík's finest, an art deco hotel in Austurvöllur Square with lovingly preserved rooms and modern art. It's a movie-star haunt where Catherine Deneuve stayed when she came to visit Björk. Hótel Borg was Iceland's first luxury hotel, built by a wrestler in the 1930s and retains great wide shower heads for a serious dose of glamour.

€€€€ Hotel Holt
Bergstaðastræti 37, T552 5700, www.holt.is.
On a quiet street in central Reykjavík, this 41-roomed boutique hotel has an elegant interior and original artwork from Iceland's largest private collection. Rooms aren't the most up to date in style but it's a fantastic location and there's a gourmet restaurant onsite too.

€€€€ Hótel Klöpp
Klapparstígur 26, T511 6062, www.centerhotels.com.
Fashionable central hotel with 46 rooms and studios just off Laugavegur, the main shopping street. Modern Scandinavian design, neutral and beige colours and wooden floors. Top-floor rooms have a good view.

€€€€ Hotel Óðinsvé
Óðinstorg, T511 6200, www.hotelodinsve.is.
An elegant, well-located hotel with a good line in stuffed seabirds. The name means 'the sanctuary of Odin', the highest of the Norse gods, and its restaurant serves modern Scandinavian food. Thick carpets, polished wood and a refined ambience.

€€€€ Hotel Plaza
Aðalstraeti 4, T595 8500, www.plaza.is.
Very central location by the square near the tourist information centre. 105 well-appointed and recently refurbished rooms with tasteful modern furniture. Multi-bed and single rooms available.

€€€€ Hotel Reykjavík Centrum
Aðalstraeti 16, T514 6000, www.hotelcentrum.is.
Set over 3 buildings, the hotel has plenty of character and combines early 1900s style with modern luxury and facilities. Angular ceilings, plenty of glass and neutral colours create a feeling of space and calm. The restaurant specializes in Icelandic cuisine.

€€€€ Hotel Skjaldbreið
Laugavegur 16, T511 6060, www.centerhotels.com.
Modern, comfortable hotel in one of the city's converted stately homes. Family-run, airy and stylish, in the centre of the city with large rooms. Located on the city's main street, it's ideal for visiting the attractions but can be noisy.

€€€€ Icelandair Reykjavík Marina Hotel
Myrargata 2, T560 8000, www.icelandairhotels.com.
Bright, fun modern hotel by Reykjavík's old harbour. With stuffed puffins and plaid jostling for position amid sheepswool stools in the lobby, an array of devilish cocktails on the chalkboard in the **Slippbarinn** bar and rooms with views of the bay, it brings together some of the best aspects of the city. Family friendly, too.

€€€€ Radisson Blu 1919 Hotel
Pósthússtræti 2, T599 1000, www. radisson blu.com/1919hotel-reykjavik.
Classy central hotel in the historic building of a former shipping company, dating from 1919. Features include a grand marble staircase, sculptures and good harbour views. Rooms are immaculate with high ceilings and

flatscreen TV. The restaurant is run by an award-winning chef and serves modern world cuisine.

€€€€-€€€ Hótel Frón
Laugavegur 22a, T511 4666,
www.hotelfron.is.
Modern hotel with 54 rooms plus studio, 1- and 2-bed modern apartments. The bright studios all have kitchenettes and are stylish and fresh. There's a restaurant and bar downstairs.

€€€ Álfhóll Guesthouse
Ránargata 8, T898 1838,
www.islandia.is/alf. May-Sep only.
The friendly 'elves' house' has double rooms, single rooms, triple rooms and apartments sleeping 2-4 with bathroom and kitchenette, all well looked after and furnished in rustic style.

€€€ Fosshótel Baron
Barónsstígur 2-4, T562 3204,
www.fosshotel.is.
Bright, modern and functional 3-star hotel with en suite doubles and apartments, centrally located and with all mod cons.

€€€ Guesthouse Adam
Skólavörðustígur 42, T861 4142,
www.adam.is.
Small guesthouse close to Hallgrímskirkja with en suite rooms with kitchen facilities and a grocery store next door. Very close to the main street, purpose-built accommodation where guests are left to their own devices. Free internet for guests and car hire available.

€€€ Guesthouse Sunna
Þórsgata 26, T511 5570, www.sunna.is.
Modern family-style guesthouse in the shadow of Hallgrímskirkja with kitchen facilities and a variety of rooms, studios and apartments.

€€€ Hostel Kex
Skúlugata 28, T561 6060,
www.kexhostel.is.
This super-trendy hostel with dorms, private rooms and family rooms is owned by a group of Icelandic Premiership footballers. As well as accommodation, there's a café-bar owned by the chef of **Dill** (Reykjavík's most high-end restaurant), a barber, a school room/karaoke room and entertainment space hosting Icelandic bands. The most engaging place to stay in the city. Ask for a sea or mountain view.

€€€ Hótel Leifur Eiríksson
Skólavörðustígur 45, T562 0800,
www.hotelleifur.is.
In a great location next to the Halgrímskirkja church, so you can always find your way home. Good-value hotel with friendly staff, personal service and breakfast provided in the café/coffee bar. Comfortable and relaxed.

€€€ Metropolitan Hotel
Ránargata 4a, T511 1155,
www.metropolitan.is.
Simple modern hotel with a personal touch and particularly good-value off-peak rooms. In a quiet part of the centre of the city.

€€€ Room with a View
Laugavegur 18, T552 7262,
www.roomwithaview.is.
Sleek modern studios and apartments above Mál og Menning bookshop on the main street in the heart of town. Panoramic city views, balconies and even hot tubs.

€€ Salvation Army Guest House
Kirkjustræti 2, T561 3203,
www.guesthouse.is.

The cheapest accommodation in the centre, with single rooms, double rooms and dorm rooms sleeping 3-6 plus sleeping bag accommodation. Bathrooms are shared and it's a bit of a squeeze but fine if you're on a budget.

€ Reykjavík Backpackers
Laugavegur 28, T578 3700, www.reykjavikbackpackers.is.
Budget accommodation in the heart of the city in a very lively location. Dorms and private rooms as well as a café, tourist information centre, bike hire, camping rental and car rental offers.

€ Reykjavík Downtown Hostel
Vesturgata 17, T553 8120, www.hostel.is.
Award-winning youth hostel – part of the country's network of HI hostels – in a central spot with 4- and 10-bed dorms plus family rooms for up to 5 and double rooms with shared or private bathrooms. Car rental, bike rental and excursions arranged. Free movie nights and music.

€ Reykjavík Loft Hostel
Bankastræti 7, T553 8140, www.hostel.is.
The city's newest hostel is in a perfect central location with dorms for 4-8 people with private bathrooms, a lounge, free Wi-Fi, balcony café with great city views and regular movie nights. They can also arrange car hire, bike hire and good value excursions.

Camping and self-catering

€€€€ Castle House Apartment & Embassy Luxury Apartments
Skálholtsstígur 2a and Garðastræti 40, T511 2166, www.hotelsiceland.net.
14 apartments near the lake and city hall with lovely views and an upmarket feel. This part of Reykjavík is quiet and very desirable. All have a small kitchen, some have a balcony with views and there is a variety in terms of space, from studios to 3-bedroom apartments. Free Wi-Fi and satellite TV.

€€€€-€€€ Luna Apartments
Spítalistígur 1, T511 2800, www.luna.is.
Simple, slightly dated but well-kept family-run apartments in a 1920s house in the centre of Reykjavík with views of the pond. Studio, 1-, 2- and 3-bed apartments available, sleeping 2-10. Kitchens and Wi-Fi in all apartments.

€€€€-€€ Tower Guesthouse
Grettisgata 22c, T899 9998, www.tower.is.
Luxury apartments in a quiet part of Reykjavík, just a short walk from key attractions. All apartments have a kitchenette with dishwasher and washing machine, private bathroom and internet. Studios, 1- and 2-bed apartments available.

€€€ Apartment K
Thingholtstræti 2, T578 9850, www.apartmentk.is.
Large variety of stylish apartments dotted around the 101 district including anything from a pad next to the town's hottest bar, complete with hot tub, to a sweet corrugated-iron cottage and a rock star suite with a bed that sleeps 6. Live like a super trendy, design-orientated rock'n'roll local by booking here.

€€€ Einholt Apartments
Bolholt 2, Grettisgata 43 and Einholt 2, T517 4050, www.stay.is.
3-star apartment hotel with 3 locations across the city offering studio and 1-, 2- and 3-bed apartments all with kitchenette, maid service, laundry, Wi-Fi and parking, bookable by the night.

€€€ Home
Skulastræti 1, T898 8532,
www.this.is/home.
4 super-designed studio apartments and one super-luxury penthouse in a historic building just off Laugavegur. Owned by an Icelandic artist/designer, there are plenty of quirks and genuine Icelandic design quirks to admire. Views from the penthouse are superb.

€€€ Lighthouse Apartments
Ranargata 9, T775 0001,
www.lighthouseapartments.is.
3 private apartments with full kitchens offering the chance to live like a local in the 101 district, sleeping 4-6. All rooms have Wi-Fi and flatscreen TV with international channels.

€€€ Rey Apartments
Grettisgata 2a, T771 4600, www.rey.is.
Central apartments sleeping 1-6, all with kitchenettes and Wi-Fi. Think wooden floors, clean Scandinavian style and modern bathrooms. They also offer airport transfers and Northern Lights tours, in season.

€€€ Reykjavík Residence Hotel
Hverfisgata 45, T561 1200, www.rrhotel.is.
Stylish apartment hotel in the centre of the city with apartments sleeping 1-6 fully furnished with flatscreen TVs, Wi-Fi and rentable iPads. Traditional modern Scandinavian decor with Icelandic maps on the walls and a travel agency plus 24-hr concierge service. All apartments have a kitchenette.

Laugardalur Valley
This area is around 3 km from the city centre – about a 20-min walk – and is not a bad place to base yourself, close to the Laugardalur Valley swimming pool, Reykjavík Zoo

and the Laugar Spa. The youth hostel and campsite are particularly good if you're on a budget. If you're looking for self-catering family accommodation near Reykjavík, have a look at the websites www.farmholidays.is and www.volcanohuts.com.

€€€€ Grand Hótel Reykjavík
Sigtúni 38, 105 Reykjavík, T514 8000,
www.grand.is.
Stylish modern business-class hotel with Icelandic restaurant, bike rental and spa. Rooms range from simple budget doubles to suites with kitchenette; many also have balconies and a view of Mount Esja. Close to the open-air swimming pool.

€€€€ Hilton Nordica
Suðurlandsbraut 2, T444 5000,
www.hiltonreykjavik.com.
This large modern business hotel has a spa and travel agency in its large and stylish chrome, glass and natural wood setting. The service is excellent and its restaurant **Vox** is known for its New Nordic dishes. Rooms at the front have excellent views over Mount Esja.

€€€ 4th Floor Hotel
Laugavegur 101, T511 3030,
www.4thfloorhotel.is.
In a prime location on Laugavegur, this hotel's rooms are great for families or friends – choose singles, twins, doubles or triples or upgrade to 1- or 2-bed apartments. Spacious, modern rooms with wooden floors and kitsch zebra print fabrics that you'll either love or hate. Cheaper rooms share bathrooms; the best rooms have balconies and sea views.

€€€ Einholt Apartments
Einholt 2, T517 4050, www.stay.is.
3-star apartment hotel offering studio and 1-, 2- and 3-bed apartments with

kitchenette, maid service, laundry, Wi-Fi and parking, bookable by the night.

€€ Guesthouse 101
Laugavegur 101, T562 6101, www.iceland101.com.
Modern and spacious guesthouse with moderate-sized rooms in the centre of the city. Triple, twin, double and family rooms available. All room rates include breakfast.

€€ Hotel Klettur
Mjölnisholti 12-14, T440 1600, www.hotelklettur.is.
Smart modern 3-star hotel with 86 rooms. Book a deluxe room with balcony for great sea views. No restaurant; breakfast only. Also has a bar serving a range of Icelandic beer and a car rental agency. Good value.

€ Reykjavík Campsite
3 km from the city centre, Sundlaugavegur 32, 105 Reykjavík, T568 6944, www.reykjavikcampsite.is. 15 May-15 Sep, possibly a little earlier by arrangement with the youth hostel next door.
It also has cabins for hire, a decent laundry and toilet block, and bike hire. Prides itself on being environmentally friendly.

€ Reykjavík City Hostel
Sundlaugavegur 34, 105 Reykjavík, T553 8110, www.hostel.is.
Right next to the sports and recreation centre, this is one of the best hostels in Iceland, though not as fashionable or friendly as hostel **Kex** (see page 41). Cheerful, informed staff and 170 beds in a modern building. Dorms for 2-6 people, or private rooms with or without shared bathroom. Kitchens, laundry and table tennis. It's a 40-min walk from the centre of Reykjavík or a 10-min bus ride.

Outskirts of Reykjavík

€€€€ Icelandair Hotel Reykjavík Natura
Nautholsvegur 52, Öskjuhlíð Hill, T444 4500, www.icelandairhotels.is.
4-star hotel in a quiet wooded area about 10 mins' walk from the city centre. Shuttle buses provided. Family friendly and the only hotel in the city to have its own indoor swimming pool. Bike rental, car rental and excursions organized.

€€€€-€€ Radisson Blu Saga Hotel
Hagatorg, 107 Reykjavík, T525 9900, www.radissonblu.is.
Immense modern Radisson hotel located just beyond the city pond and the library. Scandinavian, stylish interior with all imaginable facilities, bar, restaurant and classy professional service.

Hafnarfjörður
The only good reason to stay this far from Reykjavík is the quirky **Viking** hotel.

€€€ Hotel Viking
Strandgata 56, 220 Hafnarfjörður, T565 1213, www.fjorukrain.is.
Unique accommodation in the Viking village with 29 rooms all decorated in accordance with Icelandic, Faroese and Greenlandic style.

€ Lava Hostel and Campsite
Hjallabraut 51, 220 Hafnarfjörður, T565 0900, http://lavahostel.is.
Affordable guesthouse next to Víðistaðatún sculpture garden, 1.5 km from the centre. Rooms for 2-8 people, as well as a 45-bed dorm and a campsite. Helpful staff can help with tour bookings. Facilities include kitchen, washing machines, lounge and Wi-Fi.

Restaurants

Eating out in Iceland is an expensive affair. If you're planning on splashing the cash, there are a number of top restaurants that can give you a full Icelandic experience, complete with New Nordic cuisine, local fish, lamb and lobster dishes and some of the finest food on the planet. But the culinary life in the city isn't all refined and high class: relaxed and fun sushi bars, tapas bars, burger joints and fish and chip shops make Reykjavík an interesting place to eat out, whatever your budget. Most high-end restaurants don't get going until at least 2000; café-bars in the old town are equally more lively as the night goes on, and they turn into bars.

101 Reykjavík

€€€ Argentina
Barónsstígur 11a, T551 9555, www. argentina.is. Sun-Thu 1800-2400; Fri-Sat 1730-0100.
If you're looking for meat in this city, this is the place to visit. Argentina is a darkly seductive basement restaurant serving exceptional mouth-watering steaks of all description, specializing in beef. It's the winner of numerous accolades and is recommended.

€€€ Dill
Hverfisgötu 12, T552 1522, www. dillrestaurant.is. Wed-Sat from 1800.
Iceland's leading restaurant serving New Nordic cuisine is located in the edgy **Nordic House**. Expect a menu stuffed with modernized Icelandic delights presented with a twist: the likes of scallops and sea buckthorn, lamb, celeriac and shrimp. The most highly

rated table in town – book in advance for evening meals.

€€€ Einar Ben
Veltusundi 1, T511 5090, www.einarben.is. Wed-Fri 1730-2300, Sat-Sun 1700-2300.
The place for fine dining. Set on the top floor of a 19th-century timber house with soft lighting, drapes and chandeliers. Named after one of Iceland's most famous poets. The menu features contemporary Icelandic and international cuisine with à la carte and set menus.

€€€ Humarhúsið Restaurant
Amtmannsstígur 1, T561 3303, www. humarhusid.is. Mon-Sat from 1130, Sun from 1700.
One of Reykjavík's finest seafood restaurants, specializing particularly in lobster and offering tempting dishes like pan-fried catfish with papaya salsa. The traditional wooden building adds to the intimate and warm atmosphere.

€€€ Lækjarbrekka
Bankastræti 2, T551 4430, www. laekjarbrekka.is. Daily from 1130.
Right next door to the tourist information centre on Bankastræti, this is the place for an authentic tourist experience, including plenty of traditional fish, lamb and lobster as well as rotten shark, roast puffin and grilled Minke whale. It's one of the oldest houses in Reykjavík, built in 1834, with a well-preserved and distinguished interior.

€€€ Þrir Frakkar
Baldursgata 14, T552 3939, www.3frakkar.com. Mon-Fri 1130-1430 and 1800-2200, Sat-Sun 1800-2300.
Popular Icelandic seafood restaurant specializing in local delicacies such as whale meat or puffin. Small, intimate

and very Icelandic. Free wine if you have to wait for a table. Recommended if you like fish.

€€€ Við Tjörnina
City Hall Building, Templarasund 3,
T551 8666, www.vidtjornina.is.
Daily 1200-2300.
With a prime location by the pond, this is another specialist seafood restaurant but this time with a French twist. It has a particularly large selection of wines and is regularly voted one of the city's best seafood restaurants.

€€€ VOX
Hilton Nordica Hotel, Suðurlandsbraut 2,
T444 5050, www.vox.is.
This acclaimed New Nordic restaurant is one of the hottest tickets in town, serving the likes of reindeer, lamb, smoked duck and Nordic tapas. Brunch here is the best in town, with a buffet for ISK 3750 (weekends only). Evening meals are a lot more expensive.

€€ Gandhi
Pósthússtæti17, T511 1691,
www.gandhi.is.
Indian restaurant serving mainly Keralan food with an emphasis on fish. Spices are imported directly from India; Gandhi is Iceland's first South Indian restaurant.

€€ Hornið
Hafnarstræti 15, T551 3340,
www.hornid.is. Daily 1100-2330.
Simple café-bistro serving mainly French and Mediterranean food with coffee and cakes during the day as well as pan-fried Arctic char, pizza and seafood later on.

€€ Saemundur at Hostel Kex
Skúlagata 28, T561 6060,
www.kexhostel.is. Daily 1200-2300.

This restaurant and bar is as popular with the locals as it is with those staying at the hostel, and is owned by the restaurateur behind **Dill**. Great views, good times. Expect wholesome local ingredients and daily changing menus with the likes of fish and lamb assured plus a vegetarian selection.

€€ Sjavargrillid
Skólavörðustígur 14, T571 1100, www.
sjavargrillid.is. Mon and Thu 1100-1500
and 1700-2230; Fri-Sat 1100-1500 and
1700-2330; Sun 1700-2230.
One of the best-value spots in the city to try New Nordic with puffin, whale, cormorant and sushi all on the menu.

€€ Smurstöðin
Harpa Concert Hall, Austurbakki 2, T519
9750, www.smurstodin.is/en. Mon-Wed
1000-1800, Tue and Fri 1000-2100, Sat
1000-2100, Sun 1100-1800.
Stylish new Scandinavian restaurant in the glittering concert hall featuring Danish-French light meals. Expect open sandwiches, fish and Icelandic platters of lobster, lamb and berries.

€ Jómfrúin
Lækjargata 4, T551 0100,
www.jomfruin.is. Daily 1100-1800.
Danish open-sandwich restaurant with a bistro feel. Beef and salmon sandwiches start at around ISK 1500.

€ Krúa Thai
Tryggvagata 14, T561 0039, www.
kruathai.is. Mon-Fri 1130-2130,
Sat 1200-2130, Sun 1700-2130.
Small Thai restaurant serving deep-fried fish, shrimps, chicken and all that you'd expect at unbelievable prices for this city. There's an even cheaper lunchtime special Mon-Fri costing ISK 1400 for 3 courses.

Cafés and bistros

€€ Café Paris
Austurstræti 14, T551 1020, www. cafeparis.is. Sep-Apr daily 0900-0100; May-Aug daily 0800-0100.
With the best view of Austurvöllur Square and often spilling out into the street, Café Paris is a refined café doubling as a bar with a relaxed Sun-morning atmosphere.

€ B5
Bankastræti 5, T552 9600, www.b5.is.
Trendy bistro with changing art exhibitions, a private club in the old bank vaults behind it and a burger bar. Good for coffee too.

€ Baejarins Beztu
Corner of Tryggvagata and Pósthússtræti, T511 1156, www.bbp.is.
Reykjavík's original hot dog kiosk has become something of an institution, despite its uninspiring location in a car park facing the harbour. The hot dog (*pylsur*) comes with mustard, ketchup and raw and fried onions and are very tasty.

€ Café Garðurinn
Klappurstígur 37, T561 2345. Mon-Tue, Thu-Fri 1100-2000, Wed 1100-1800, Sat 1200-1700, Sun closed.
Small vegetarian café/restaurant with a daily selection of home-cooked vegetarian specialities, soup, sandwiches, coffee, tea and cakes.

€ Grái Kötturinn
Hverfisgata 16a, T551 1544. Mon-Fri 0700-1500, Sat 0800-1500.
A bohemian 1950s-style diner with bookshop chic. 'The Grey Cat', named after a cat that once lived in the building, is run by artists and serves large plates

of hangover-style fry-ups and pancakes, great for brunch.

€ Icelandic fish and chips
Tryggvagata 11, T511 1118, www. fishandchips.is. Daily 1200-2100.
The Icelandic take on the Brit tradition includes the freshest fish imaginable battered in spelt and barley and with an accompanying mayonnaise-like dip made from *skyr* in flavours including ginger and wasabi. Even the chips are hand roasted with rosemary. Really worth checking out whether you're on a budget or not.

€ Islenskibarinn
Ingólfsstræti 1a, T517 6767, http://islenskibarinn.is/net, www.isklenskibarinn.is. Sun-Thu 1130-0100, Fri-Sat 1130-0300; kitchen open daily 1130-2200.
Icelandic bar-bistro that is always good for a taste of Iceland. Sample menu items include seared minke whale, lamb terrine and salt cod; lunch starts at ISK 990.

€ The Laundromat Café
Austurstræti 9, T587 7555, www. thelaundromatcafe.com. Mon-Thu 0800-2400, Fri 0800-0100, Sat 0900-0100, Sun 0900-2400.
This retro 1950s café-bar is a particularly popular spot for brunch at the weekend, and has colour-coded books wrapped around the bar, colourful world maps on the wall and a laundrette and children's play area downstairs.

€ Mokka Kaffi
Skólavörðustígur 3a, T552 1174, www.mokka.is. Daily 0900-1830.
The oldest café in town, dating from 1958, Mokka is an intimate art gallery/café serving the best waffles in town. A quiet refuge popular with the locals.

€ Noodle Station
Skólavörðustígur 21a, T551 3199.
Mon-Fri 1100-2200, Sat-Sun 1200-2200.
Tiny noodle bar serving just 3 dishes:
noodle soup with beef, noodle soup
with chicken and vegetarian noodle
soup. Noodle bars have become the fast
food bar of choice in the city and this
one is the best.

€ Sea Baron
Geirsgata 8, T553 1500, www.saegreifinn.is.
May-Aug 1130-2300; Sep-Apr 1130-2200.
This old shack in the old harbour village
is as down and dirty as it gets. Sit on
an old plastic oil drum beneath artfully
draped fishing nets and enjoy the best
lobster soup in town. There are no
airs and graces but that soup sure is
good. They also serve grilled skewered
marinaded fish including whale, halibut,
sole, smoked eel and catfish.

€ Te og Kaffi
Laugavegur, Skólavörðustígur,
Lækjartorg, Austurstræti,
www.teogkaffi.is.
Iceland's answer to Starbucks, this chain
is all over town. The coffee is good – not
the cheapest in town though – and the
shops also sell a range of tea, coffee and
stylish crockery.

€ Tíu Dropar
Laugavegur 27, T551 9380, www.
facebook.com/TiuDropar. Mon-Fri
0900-0100, Sat-Sun 1000-0100.
Cosy Icelandic basement café below the
main street serving toasted sandwiches,
soups and pancakes. Tiu Dropar is an
Icelandic phrase for a cup of coffee –
'10 drops'.

Outskirts of Reykjavík

€€€ Perlan Öskjuhlíð
105 Reykjavík, Öskjuhlíð Hill, T562 0200,
www.perlan.is. Daily from 1800.
Highly rated Icelandic restaurant serving
meat and seafood to distinguished
diners with a slowly revolving floor
and beautiful views of the city. Serves
lobster, veal, beef, lamb and even grilled
reindeer. Almost prohibitively expensive
even by Icelandic standards.

€€ Nauthóll Bistro
Nauthólsvegur 106, Nauthólsvík Beach,
T599 6660, http://nautholl.is.
Daily 1100-2200.
A little out of town but well worth a visit.
The only turf-roofed café in town, down
by the geothermal beach and woods
by the Pearl; cosy and warm inside. The
slabs of chocolate cake are delicious as
are the seafood salads.

Hafnarfjörður

€€€ Fjörukráin
Viking Village, Strandgata 50a,
220 Hafnarfjörður, T565 1213,
www.fjorukrain.is. Sun-Thu
1200-0100, Fri-Sat 1200-0300.
Eat as much as you can in the Viking
hall of Fjörukráin where traditional
Viking feasts of lamb, lobster and shark
are served up in a large hall on shared
tables. A bit of a pantomime but fun if
you like that kind of thing. Downstairs in
the cave bar you can sign up to be fake
kidnapped by the Vikings too.

Bars and clubs

For a town this size, Reykjavík's nightlife holds its own. With over 120 bars and clubs, there's always somewhere to party.

Fri and Sat nights are the wildest nights here, and that means serious clubbing from around 2400 to 0800 in the morning. The bars and clubs don't really fill up until after midnight. Those drinking in the bars and cafés before midnight are mainly tourists as the expense of drinking all night encourages many of the locals to drink heavily at home before heading into town. Then to round it all off when the bars and clubs have closed, head for Austurvöllur Square where people tend to hang around. Coffee and lots of it are the order of the day on Sun.

The long summer days and yawning winter nights give a whole new twist to the concept of partying till dawn. Follow the crowd for a lively night; it's typical for bars to stay open as long as people are still drinking at the weekends, or alternatively close if no one's around. Music-wise you'll find a little bit of nearly everything in the city, from golden oldies to innumerable DJ sets and a few retro bars. The annual **Iceland Airwaves** music festival, held in the autumn, brings crowds of revelers to the city and sees music played in bars, hotels, museums and the Blue Lagoon among other unique spots. It's wise to book ahead at this time as accommodation regularly sells out.

The traditional Icelandic weekend pastime is the *runtur* or pub crawl, primarily along Laugavegur with detours off it to the best bars and clubs with DJ sets the order of the day.

Reykjavíkurs have only had legal access to beer since 1989 and there are many unusual things about drinking in the city even today. In common with other Scandinavian countries, alcohol is state-controlled, expensive and, outside of bars and restaurants, can only be bought from the **Vinbuðin** shops. Pick up a copy of *The Grapevine*, www.grapevine.is, to see what's on and to find out which bars have a happy hour when. Their 'appy hour' app available for iPhones and the like also guides you through the cheapest times to drink in the city's bars.

101 Reykjavík

Bakkhus
Tryggvagata 22, T578 3200.
Bar/club with foosball, cheap beer, vodka, dancing and regular film nights and live music.

Café Rósenberg
Klapparstígur, T551 2442, www.facebook. com/pages/Café-Rosenberg.
The closest thing that Reykjavík has to a jazz club, with old instruments on the walls and live jazz or blues. People come here to check out new bands and chat rather than to dance. Ask at the bar for the programme.

Dillon Whiskey Bar
Laugavegur 30, T511 2400, www. facebook.com/DillonWhiskeyBar. Mon-Thu 1400-0100. Fri-Sat 1400-0300, Sun 1400-0100.
Rock bar in an old house on the main street with regular small rock gigs on its tiny stage and a vast selection of whiskey.

Dolly
Hafnarstræti 4. Wed-Thu 2000-0100, Fri-Sat 2000-0430.

Hip bar playing electro and dance, up there with the most trendy bar/clubs in the city.

Harlem
Tryggvagata 22, T571 8180. Sun-Thu 1800-0100, Fri-Sat 1800-0430.
Bar/club playing electronica with occasional events and DJ sets.

Kaffibarinn
Bergstaðstræti 1, T551 1588, www.facebook.com/kaffibarinn. Mon-Thu 1500-0100, Fri-Sat 1500-0400, Sun 1500-0100.
One of Reykjavík's hippest hangouts for artists and musicians. Blur's Damon Albarn is said to have a stake in this small corrugated-iron-clad 2-storey bar. It's laid-back and inviting. Upstairs, old sofas and tables upstairs add a touch of bohemian glamour.

The Lebowski Bar
Laugavegur 20a, T552 2300, www.lebowskibar.is. Sun-Thu 1130-0100, Fri-Sat 1130-0400.
Diner and bowling alley celebrating the great bowling film *The Big Lebowski*. Good for burgers, chat and drinking late at the weekend.

Microbar
Austurstraeti 6, T847 9084. Sun-Sat 1600-2400.
The only place in the city to drink Icelandic microbrews, exotic draft beers and liquor. Judged the best in town.

Prikið
Bankastræti 12, T551 3366, http://prikid.is. Mon-Fri 0800-0100, Fri 0800-0430, Sat 1200-0430, Sun 1200-0100.
The oldest place to party, Prikið means 'the stick' and is a fetchingly small and cosy pub, ideal for starting your evening. Expect everyone from the young and hip to old men reading newspapers in the corner. Standing room only at weekends.

Slippbarinn
Icelandair Reykjavík Marina Hotel, Myrargata 2, T560 8080, www.slippbarinn.is.
This stylish bar has a great sense of fun and an even better cocktail list. A good place to start the night.

Vegamót
Vegamotastig 4, T511 3040, www.vegamot.is. Happy hour Thu-Sat 2200-0100.
Elegant bar-bistro with 2 floors. As the night progresses the atmosphere starts to change and the crowd with it as Vegamót evolves into a nightclub with Icelandic DJ sets.

Entertainment

Despite its size, Reykjavík has a thriving arts scene and you should always be able to find something interesting to do or see. Much of the arts season is focused on the winter as Reykjavíkurs make use of the sunlight when it's there to spend time outdoors. This means that the National Theatre is in recess during the summer – when most tourists are here.

Icelanders visit the cinema more times per person than any other nationality, around 5 times a year, and you'll find a number of cinemas in the city centre. Films are shown in the original language with Icelandic subtitles.

It's contemporary music, above all, that is the live current running through the city all year round. Sung in both English and Icelandic, it fuses with the nightlife as one of the most popular attractions of the city. The city hosts yearly music, film and cultural festivals towards the end of the summer, see Festivals on page 53. Pick up a copy of the English-speaking newspaper *Grapevine* or look online at www.grapevine.is to get an idea of what's on, or drop into the tourist office or youth hostel for a daily list of what's on and where.

Cinema

In recent years Iceland's cinematic output has been staggering. Anything from art house movies to Tom Cruise and Morgan Freeman-fronted blockbuster *Oblivion*, Russell Crowe's *Noah* and Ben Stiller's *The Secret Life of Walter Mitty*. TV series *Game of Thrones* was also filmed in the wilds of north Iceland. The Icelandic light and general atmosphere lends a special quality to anything filmed out here – and it helps that the days are so long and light in the summer, and that the government offers a 20% tax rebate to directors on the production costs incurred in the country. When it comes to watching films, the art house cinema on Hverfisgata is a good place to catch an actual Icelandic film (with English subtitles usually); if you're looking for a mainstream hit, try **Kringlan** shopping mall. The website www.whatson.is is also useful.

There are 5 cinemas in Reykjavík, mainly showing American movies in English with subtitles.

Bioparadis, *Hverfisgata 52, T412 7711, www.bioparadis.is.* Art house cinema showing cult classics and Icelandic films. Evening showings only.

Háskólabió, *Hagatorg, 107 Reykjavík, T530 1919, www.haskolabio.is.* Standard multiplex.

Sambió, *Álfabakki 8, 101 Reykjavík, T587 8900, www.sambio.is.* Standard multiplex.

Sambió, *Kringlan 4-12, 103 Reykjavík, T588 0800.* Standard multiplex.

Sambió, *Smáralind shopping centre, Kópavogur, T564 0000, www.haskolabio.is.* Standard multiplex.

Volcano Cinema, *Volcano House, Tryggvagata 11, 101 Reykjavík, T555 1900, www.volcanohouse.is. Daily 1000-2100; film starts on the hour, every hour and takes 40 mins.* Want to find out more about volcanoes? This documentary will tell you all, covering the Eyjafjallajökull eruption of 2010 and the larger and more devastating 1973 eruption in the Westman Islands south of Reykjavík. There's also a café, souvenir shop and Icelandic fish and chips on site.

Dance

Iceland Dance Company, *Listabraut 3, 103 Reykjavík, T588 0900, www.id.is.* Small company based at the Reykjavík City Theatre (see Theatre, below), focusing exclusively on modern and contemporary dance. They work closely with other Icelandic artists and have commissioned music from everyone from rap group Quarashi to low-fi ambient group Múm. Highly regarded in their field.

Jazz

There isn't a main jazz venue in Reykjavík and you may have to hunt it out only to find a very modern version of what you're looking for. As with rock and pop, keep an eye out as things change and concerts can happen anywhere. A low-key jazz festival is held in the city at the beginning of Oct.

Café Rósenberg, *Klapparstigur, T551 2442.* This café/bar has old instruments on the walls and often has live bands playing jazz and blues.

Reykjavík City of Literature

Books tell a lot about a nation. Iceland publishes more books per head that almost anywhere else in the world – showing that a literary culture is alive and kicking in this creative, thoughtful country. The strange thing is that while about five books are published for every thousand Icelanders (far more than anywhere else) Icelandic literature hasn't really reached the mainstream outside the country – yet. Sure, back in 1955, Halldor Laxnes was awarded the Nobel Prize for Literature for his novel *Independent People* about the struggles and poverty of a sheep farmer in the wilds of Iceland, and his many novels are available in translation, but there's not yet a modern blockbuster writer that is recognized the world over, like, for example, Sweden's Stieg Larsson.

In August 2011, Reykjavík was designated a UNESCO City of Literature. The award recognizes the city's outstanding literary history tracing back to the Sagas and ancient medieval literature, as well as the large role that literature plays in Icelandic life today.

Within the modern Scandinavian crime genre, there are a couple of Icelanders to watch out for. Despite the low rates of crime in the country, writers Yrsa Sigurdardottir and Arnaldur Indridason, who has won the Golden Dagger Award, have achieved some fame abroad, especially in Germany, and are translated into English. These more recent books take place in Reykjavík and give a bit of an insight into modern life here.

Looking back further in time, it's hard not to think that some of the Icelandic crime writers have been influenced by what went before them. Way before

Jómfrúin, *Lækjargata, T551 0100, www.jomfruin.is.* Daily 1100-1800. Has occasional mid-afternoon sessions in the summer.

Music

Icelandic music has gradually been making its way across the Atlantic and suddenly, radios are playing singles from the likes of Of Monsters and Men as well as Björk, Sigur Ros and Jónsi.

Iceland Airwaves is the pinnacle of the musical calendar in the city, a week-long music festival held in the autumn when bars, clubs, cafés, museums and even swimming pools hosts the country's most up-and-coming acts, bookended with stellar artists from the

USA, UK and Europe. There are also a number of venues in the city where you can find live music nearly every night of the week, and certainly at the weekend.

Harpa concert hall has brought a new dimension to the music scene in Reykjavík, with regular classical concerts plus touring acts of world-class calibre taking to its 3 stages.

Harpa, *Austurbakki 2, T528 5000, www. harpa.is.* Olafur Eliasson-designed showpiece concert hall hosting classical and modern concerts, opera from the Icelandic Opera and orchestral performances from the Icelandic Symphony Orchestra. Worth a visit if you're interested in architecture too.

them, in the Middle Ages, the Icelandic settlers recorded stories of myth and fable and life on the land on calfskin manuscripts. Some deal with brutal criminals, bad behaviour and Viking-era drama – and all are very colourful. The Icelandic Sagas have been widely translated into English and remain a pretty good read. If you're starting out, Egil's Saga or Njal's Saga are among the most accessible.

The vellum manuscripts themselves are on view at the Culture House where guided talks and tours are available in English. Among them is the *Codex Regius* from AD 1270, notable because of the stories told within it concerning Norse mythology. It's where our modern day understanding of these times comes from. Plenty of museum and tourist shops sell the sayings of the Vikings in book form too – and those about lifestyle, treating guests and how to behave properly still ring true today. They certainly challenge the notion of the Vikings as bloodthirsty savages.

The city holds a biannual Literature Festival, which has been attended by writers including Kurt Vonnegut and Seamus Heaney, and there is a biannual **International Children's Literature Festival** in the capital too. The City Library hosts literature walks and poetry happenings take place in many of the regular festivals and events in the city through the year.

As an international city of literature, Reykjavík now has a responsibility to further promote Iceland's writers, writing and reading. The international airport is decorated with quotes from Icelandic writers and verses of Icelandic poetry are painted on the pavements. There are plans afoot for benches in the city to become literary retreats where Icelandic literature can be enjoyed in translation via smart phones.

Theatre

If you arrive in Reykjavík in the summer the options for experiencing Icelandic theatre are limited, mainly because the National Theatre has its annual break at this time. At other times of year, drama in the city varies according to supply and demand, and the National Theatre in particular can show anything from Shakespeare and Chekhov to West End musicals and opera. **Harpa** (above) also has occasional theatrical performances and a tourist-orientated stand up show called *How to become Icelandic in 60 minutes*.

National Theatre, *Hverfisgata 19, 101 Reykjavík, T551 1200, www.leikhusid. is/english. Box office open Tue-Sun 1300-1800, and until 2000 on days of performance.* Information about the programme can be found at the tourist information centre.

Reykjavík City Theatre, *Listabraut 3, Kringlan, 103 Reykjavík, T568 8000, www.borgarleikhus.is.* Quirkier theatrical offerings plus a wide range of children's theatre.

Festivals

Traditional celebrations were once at the heart of the Icelandic community, providing a reason to get together and promote a feeling of nationhood against the backdrop of isolated farmsteads. Nowadays the traditional feasts, featuring marching bands and lots of dried cod, still survive alongside a host of modern festivals heralding the new identity of the country.

Perhaps the most notable of these celebrations is the **Iceland Airwaves**, which brings together the best UK and US bands and mixes them up with local bands to develop a devastatingly cool line up. And Iceland being Iceland, the festival calendar includes everything from the sublime to the ridiculous: from a day spent eating cream buns to what has been dubbed the best festival in the world. This extravaganza takes place on Heimaey in the Westman Islands on the 1st weekend in Aug, when 10,000 people come together camp, drink, party and drink some more, recovering the next day to catch baby puffins and send them out to sea until they get bigger. How refreshingly different.

1 Jan New Year's Day (1st) A national holiday when almost everything closes and Icelanders recover from the excesses of the night before. Fireworks and bonfires take place into the long dark night the evening before.

Feb Winter Festival A 3-day festival held in Reykjavík to celebrate the winter. It's also called **Festival of Light** and features a vast array of art and cultural projects around the theme of lights, to compensate for the lack of it.

Feb Thorrablot Ancient food festival where restaurants across Reykjavík serve historical food: fermented skate, rotten shark, whey-cured meat and fish and fermented bull's testicles.

24 Feb Bun Day 3 days of celebrations beginning with the eating of cream buns.

25 Feb Bursting Day Meat dishes are eaten till people are fit to burst.

Feb Food and Fun Festival Annual week-long food festival at the end of the month, featuring national and international chefs.

Mar Design March Celebration of Icelandic Design 4 days of openings, exhibitions and workshops plus talk about fonts, fashion and furniture design. Check www.icelanddesign.is for details.

20 Mar Spring Equinox No celebrations but it marks the moment when the hours of daylight finally equal those of darkness.

Easter Holy Thursday Marks the start of the Easter holidays and a 5-day weekend. Most business, banks and shops are closed.

Apr Dead Week Students preparing to take their graduate exams parade around the streets dressed up in costumes.

1st Thu after 18 Apr First Day of Summer A public holiday and a time of celebrations and parades, even though it still feels like winter.

1 May Labour Day A public holiday celebrated by an annual parade around the city centre.

May Reykjavík Arts Festival An annual 2-week festival promoting Icelandic and international culture with exhibitions, concerts, theatre, dance and opera performances.

1st weekend in Jun Festival of the Sea Annual event centring around the harbour, based on an old Icelandic tradition to honour those who make their living from the sea. There are numerous cultural activities, parades, arts and crafts activities for kids, food fairs and sailing competitions.

17 Jun Icelandic National Day The day when Icelanders celebrate becoming a republic with an explosion of red, blue and white colours. When power moved from Denmark back to the country in 1944, the birth date of the leader of the independence movement Jón Sigurdsson was chosen as the day for celebration.

21 Jun Summer Solstice The longest day of the year. The sun rises at 0254 and doesn't set until 2404.

2nd weekend in Aug   Gay Pride Originally invented to fight for gay people's rights, this annual event draws visitors from far and wide. Thousands of people gather to march through the streets of Reykjavík. Celebrations include an outdoor concert with Icelandic and international artists, with dancing and other activities.

3rd weekend in Aug   Reykjavík Cultural Night and Marathon Associated with the birthday of the city, all sorts of celebrations take place late into the night with music and fireworks taking centre stage. The Reykjavík marathon is held during the day with thousands of people of all ages taking part.

Sep Reykjavík Film Festival Screenings of Icelandic and international films, particularly arthouse movies. Runs during Sep and Oct. See www.riff.is for details.

9 Oct-8 Dec Imagine Peace Tower This work of art by Yoko Ono remembers John Lennon, a tower of light emanating from Viðey Island, remembering his birthday and the day of his death.

Mid-Oct Iceland Airwaves 4 days of celebrating Icelandic rock and pop music with a few international appearances amid the local talent. Venues include the Blue Lagoon. For details visit www.icelandairwaves.com.

1 Dec Independence Day Anniversary of the day in 1918 when Iceland was granted home rule from Denmark. It's a bank holiday throughout the country.

21 Dec Winter Solstice The shortest day of the year. The sun rises at 1122 and sets at 1530, barely skimming the horizon.

23 Dec Þorláksmessa This day pays tribute to St Þorlákur, one of the few indigenous saints of Iceland. Shops are open until 2300 for last-minute Christmas shopping.

25 Dec Christmas Day A public holiday. Many Icelanders visit family and friends and celebrate with festive food. The city is illuminated through the whole month with Christmas lights, a Christmas market and the 13 Christmas Lads (the country's equivalent to Father Christmas) along with the Christmas Whale, the Christmas Cat and an old ogress who eats children, called Grylla.

31 Dec New Year's Eve Icelanders say goodbye to the old year with an enormous firework displays and bonfires which illuminate the sky at midnight. Tour companies www.re.is and www.adventure.is can offer guided tours of the city and its bonfires.

Shopping

Fans of Scandinavian design with bottomless wallets will be in heaven here. Laugavegur, Reykjavík's main high street, is lined with boutiques selling the type of thing that you'd expect to see on Lady Gaga, while tourist shops sell anything from volcanic rocks to traditional knitted jumpers, the *lopipeysa*.

Shopping malls like **Smáralind** in Kópavogur and **Kringlan** have English, European and American shops, though goods are more expensive than those you'll find on Laugavegur, the main shopping street in the city. Shops are generally open Mon-Sat 1000-1700, with the exception of the out-of-town malls and supermarkets and **Mál og Menning** bookshops, which are open late, and **Kolaportið**, the town flea market, which is open on Sun.

Arts and crafts

Kraum, *Aðalstræti 10, http://kraum.is*. A design hub and retail outlet representing more than 200 Icelandic artists. Said to be the oldest wooden building in the city. Sells everything from wooden toys and jewellery, to clothing and ceramics.

Bookshops

Mál og Menning, *Laugavegur 18, T580 5000, Bankastræti 2, and Kringlan Mall, www.bmm.iswww.malogmenning.is*. Exceptional Icelandic chain with a full range of books in English and other languages on Iceland and textbooks for learning Icelandic. The Laugavegur branch has a café upstairs and is open until 2200.

Peninn Eymundsson, *Austurstræti 18, 110 Reykjavík, T540 2000, www.penninn.is*. Has an excellent selection of maps, magazines and souvenirs as well as a large selection of English-language books.

Clothes

66° North, *Bankastræti 9, T517 6020, www.66north.com*. If you do enjoy adventuring and need to get kitted out with the best gear, head here. 66° North sells padded jackets, balaclavas, socks, gloves and anything else you might need in this often cold and inhospitable island.

Cintamani, *Bankastræti, also at Smaralind and Kringlan, www.cintamani.is*. The country's other main outdoor clothing supplier with the slogan 'Iceland's dress code'. It's a little more urban than 66° North.

Geysir, *Skólavörðustígur 16, T519 6000, www.geysirshops.is*. Gorgeous Icelandic and Nordic clothes store stocking the likes of Fjallravenkanken, Farmers Market and Gant as well as Levis. Look out for sheepskin rugs, sealskins and the designer woolen collection by Vik Prjonsdottir that includes the Icelandic beard cap and a seal-shaped knitted onesie. Upscale outdoor gear that looks just as good if you opt to stay in.

Jewellery

Aurum Design and Lifestyle, *Bankastraeti 4, T551 2770, www.aurum.is. Mon-Fri 1000-1800, Sat 1100-1700, Sun 1200-1700*. Lifestyle shop selling Japanese and Icelandic design items for the home with a lovely Icelandic jewellery shop added on selling precious metals and uniquely Icelandic items.

Markets

Kolaportið, *Tryggvagötu 19, T562 5030, www.kolaportid.is. Sat-Sun 1100-1700*. In Kolaportið flea market you'll find a host of bric-a-brac stalls, second-hand clothing and a wide range of Icelandic books. One look at the stalls and you won't be surprised to find that the Icelanders publish more books per head than any other nation. There are also a few souvenir and craft stalls that are markedly less expensive and more interesting than the shops in town. Towards the back of the hall is the main event – the fish market. You can try the famous *hákarl* as well as dried fish, huge fresh fulmar eggs and a lot of fish cheaper than at the supermarket. Unlike the majority of places in Reykjavík, you'll need cash to buy from the stalls, but there's a handy ATM by the toilets near the east entrance.

Photography
Reykjavík Foto, *Laugavegur 51, T577 5900, www.reykjavikfoto.is. Mon-Fri 1100-1800, Sat 1100-1600*. City centre store that sells everything you might need if you're going out to capture the Northern Lights or other Icelandic delights on film: cameras, lenses, film and iPhones too.

Shopping malls
Kringlan Mall, *112-150 Kringlumýrarbraut, 105 Reykjavík, on the outskirts of Reykjavík, about a 30-min walk from 101 toward Perlan, T17 9000, www.kringlan.is. Mon-Wed 1000-1830, Thu 1000-2100, Fri 1000-1900, Sat 1000-1800, Sun 1300-1800. Free bus from tourist information centre at Aðalstræti 2, May-Sep Mon-Sat every hour 1000-1700; Sun 1300-1600*. It's got a very different atmosphere from the shopping street in downtown Reykjavík with a number of chain fashion and homeware stores from Europe. It also has an off-licence, or *vínbúðin*. There's also a bookshop and a post office and the 3rd floor is home to a load of fast-food outlets, mainly American, and the toilets. The cinema and restaurants are open later in the evening and at weekends.

Supermarkets
There are a number of supermarkets in the centre of Reykjavík if you're self-catering. Try **10-11** on Austurstræti, **Bónus**, on Laugavegur, and **Hagkaup**, which is a lot larger, at Kringlan Mall (see above).

What to do

Bike hire
A number of hotels and hostels in Reykjavík offer bike hire as do the following:
Bike Company, *Faxafeni 8, 108 Reykjavik, T665 5600, www.bikecompany.is. Jun-Aug daily 0800-2100; Sep-May Mon-Sat 0900-1900*. Also has branches at the **Icelandic Travel Market**, Bankastræti 2, and **Trip**, Laugavegur 54. Stocks a full range of bikes and runs guided tours through scenic valleys, the highlands and the city.
Reykjavík Bike Tours and Bicycle Rental, *Aegisgarður, T694 8956, www.icelandbike.com*. As well as offering bike hire, the company also runs guided bike tours of the city, cycling tours to and around the Golden Circle, Westman Isles and Blue Lagoon. They stock a full range of mountain bikes plus helmets with options of child bike seats and trailers for families. Private tours also available.

Day tours
If you're in the city for a short visit, these companies run reliable coach tours to the key sights around the city with commentary.
Arctic Adventures, *Laugavegur 11, T562 7000, www.adventures.is*. Trekking, horse riding, sightseeing, glacier tours, caving, kayaking and hiking. Mainly in jeeps and smaller groups.
Iceland Excursions, *Harfnarstræti 20, 101 Reykjavík, T540 1313, www.icelandexcursions.is*. Day bus tours and activities including bus trips to Gullfoss, Jokulasarlon, the Blue Lagoon, whale watching, horse riding and Northern Lights tours.
Reykjavík Excursions, *BSÍ Bus Terminal, 101 Reykjavík, T580 5400, ww.re.is*. Day bus tours and activities including bus trips to Gullfoss, Geysir, the Blue Lagoon, whale

Family-friendly Reykjavík

Iceland is a very family friendly place once you get past the price tag. There are a number of great things to do with children that don't cost the earth; here are just a few of them.

Swim in a thermal pool Reykjavík's thermal pools cost next to nothing and are a great introduction to family life in the city. The best for families is the open-air pool at Laugardalslaug in Laugardalur Valley, and the Blue Lagoon is great too.

Feed the ducks and geese at the pond The city's pond Tjörnin is a popular spot for kids, particularly preschoolers who like to feed the ducks and geese. There's also a playground in the park at the far end of the pond.

Get to know the Vikings Depending on the age of your children, you might like to visit the Viking museum at the Pearl; the 871 +/-2 exhibition in the centre of the city; or the camp-as-you-like Viking Village in Hafnarfjörður.

Go whale and puffin spotting The spring, summer and autumn are good times to take a whale-watching trip from Reykjavík's old harbour, and July and August are great months to spot puffins.

Visit the zoo and botanical gardens If you have toddlers who need to let off energy, the small petting zoo and botanical gardens in Laugardalur Valley are an ideal space to do just that.

Meet the Icelandic ponies Horseback tours and pony trekking are available from the stables around Reykjavík where you can get out in the fresh air and meet some of the country's most engaging inhabitants.

Wonder at nature Iceland's immense outdoors appeal is as enticing for kids as it is adults. Geysir, Gullfoss, Þingvellir and the Blue Lagoon are all great places to wonder at nature on a day trip from the city.

Watch the Northern Lights Between October and March, you can see the Northern Lights from various spots just outside the city. Sign up for a tour or ask at the tourist information centre for a good location – older children will love it.

Get arty at Kjarvalsstaðir This art gallery has a children's workshop as well as beautiful paintings by Iceland's beloved nature painter, Kjarval.

Climb Mount Esja Get some well-needed exercise with a walk up Reykjavík's closest mountain, with fantastic views from the top.

Go elf-spotting in Hafnarfjörður This Reykjavík suburb is said to have a high population of *huldufólk* or hidden people, as well as plenty of elves. The tourist information centre even has a map you can follow to locate them.

Have a coffee break at The Old Laundromat Because parents need a break too. This funky downtown café has a kids' play area downstairs and is very family friendly.

watching, super jeep tours and Northern Lights tours. Also runs the long-distance bus service around Iceland.

Diving

Dive.is, *Hólmaslóð 2, 101 Reykjavík, T578 6200, www.dive.is*. Specialist company running diving and snorkelling tours in Iceland, specializing in the Silfra Rift and offering midnight sun snorkelling and diving as well as combination tours with the Blue Lagoon, sightseeing and horse riding.

Iceland Excursions, *Harfnarstræti 20, 101 Reykjavík, T540 1313, www. icelandexcursions.is*. Tour company also offering fissure diving at Silfra and snorkelling.

Dog sledding

Dog Sledding, *T863 6733, www. dogsledding.is*. Runs glacier tours in winter and summer with beautiful blue-eyed Greenland husky dogs or skidoos. 1-hr tours in South Iceland cost from ISK 16,000. Pick-up from Reykjavík available; warm suits provided.

Fishing

Elding Whale Watching, *Ægisgardur 5, T519 5000, www.elding.is. May-Sep*. Offers sea angling tours from the old harbour in the centre of Reykjavík.

Reykjavík Angling Club, *Rafstöðvarvegi 14, 101 Reykjavík, T568 6050, www.svfr.is*. The central angling club and offers permits, advice and maps of the best fishing areas.

Veiðihornið, *Siðimuli 8, 108 Reykjavík, T568 8410, www.veidihornid.is*. The main fishing shop in Reykjavík selling permits and offering advice about freshwater fishing.

Glacier hiking

Arctic Adventures, *Laugavegur 11, T562 7000, www.adventures.is*. Adventure tour company offering glacier hikes.

Iceland Touring Association, *Mörkin 6, T568 2533, www.fi.is*. As well as offering advice, the ITA operates a number of mountain huts where hikers can stay in sleeping-bag accommodation (book in advance). It also offers a variety of tours including hiking and cross-country skiing.

Icelandic Mountain Guides, *Stórhöfði 33, 101 Reykjavík, T587 9999, www.mountainguide.is*. Runs summer tours around Skaftafell National Park in southeast Iceland and tours from Reykjavík to Sólheimajökull glacier, Hengill geothermal area and Heiðmörk Nature Reserve. Also runs climbing, backpacking and polar expeditions on request. For the Laugavegurinn walk from Landmannalaugar, see page 79.

Mountain Guides/Iceland Rovers, *c/o Bankastræti 2, 101 Reykjavík, T587 9999, www.mountainguides.is, www. icelandrovers.is*. Award-winning local specialists in glacier walking tours.

Golf

Play in the midnight sun on a course beside a lava field where the sand pit is black volcanic sand. It's like nothing else in the world. Iceland has 65 golf courses and several around Reykjavík. Midnight golf is available in the summer.

Golf Iceland, *Engjavegur 6, 104 Reykjavík, T514 4050, www.golficeland.org*.

Helicopter tours

Helicopter.is, *Reykjavík Domestic Airport, T562 2500, www.helicopter.is*. Helicopter tours of Iceland from Reykjavík including bathing in hot springs, picnicking on glaciers and sunset flights. A range of package tours from 30 mins to 3 hrs are available as well as customized tours.

Horse riding

Eldhestar, *Völlum, 810 Hveragerði, T480 4800, www.eldhestar.is*. Just 30 mins from Reykjavík, this stables can pick up at your hotel and take your on a variety of riding tours from 2-hr to 7-day tours around the glaciers, lava fields and volcanos.

Islenski Hesturinn, *Sturlugata 3, 110 Reykjavík, T434 7979, http://islenski hesturinn.is*. The Icelandic Horse stables offer trips in the volcanic landscape surrounding Reykjavík.

Laxnes Horse Farm, *271 Laxnesi, Mosfellsbæ, T566 6179, www.laxnes.is*. A large range of tours start here from this stable just north of Reykjavík: 7-day tours to Landmannalaugar, Golden Circle tours and even whale watching and horseback combinations. It's a lovely part of the country for a horse ride.

Knitting

Knitting Iceland, *3rd floor, Laugavegur 25, T497 1770, www.esjatravel.is/en*. Knitting tours include accommodation, teaching and some excursions. Not perhaps the most obvious choice, this company runs knitting tours where you can learn to knit a shawl or *lopi* – traditional Icelandic jumper – in combination with other activities.

Northern Lights

Tours cost around ISK 5000. See also box, page 11.

Arctic Adventures, *Laugavegur 11, T562 7000, www.adventures.is*. Extensive Northern Lights adventure tours into the highlands of Iceland, with lava cave excursions, in a super jeep with maximum 8 other guests.

Iceland Excursions, *Harfnarstræti 20, 101 Reykjavík, T540 1313, www.icelandexcursions.is. Operates tours 15 Sep-15 Apr*. Offers bus tours to see the Northern Lights outside the city.

Reykjavík Excursions, *BS Í Bus Terminal, 101 Reykjavík, T580 5400, www.re.is. Oct-Mar only*. Bus tours to see the Northern Lights around Reykjavík.

Quad bikes

Quad biking has taken off as a great way to see the lava fields in an adrenalin-fuelled way, just outside the city. Most companies will pick up in the centre.

Iceland Excursions, *Harfnarstræti 20, 101 Reykjavík, T540 1313, www.icelandexcursions.is*. ATV or quad-bike tours on the Reykjanes Peninsula lava fields near the Blue Lagoon and a soothing swim afterwards. Also off-roading and volcano safaris by quad bike.

Safari Quads, *Lambhagavegur, 113 Reykjavik, T821 1311, www.quad.is*. Tours include New Year's safaris, mountain safaris, night rides and extreme exploration near Mosfellsbaer/Mount Esja. Combined tours with caving, horse riding and snorkelling also available.

Skiing

The ski areas of Bláfjoll and Skalafell are both 25 mins from the city, with ski rental and lessons on weekends. Visit www.skidasvaedi.is for more information.

Snowmobiling

Iceland Excursions, *Harfnarstræti 20, 101 Reykjavík, T540 1313, www.icelandexcursions.is*. Offers tours on Langjökull glacier combined with super jeep tours of the Golden Circle.

Mountaineers of Iceland, *Skutuvogi 12E, 104 Reykjavík, T580 9900, www.mountaineers.is*. Day tours and tailor-made programmes with snowmobile tours, monster trucks and more.

Spa

For Blue Lagoon, see page 64.
Laugar Spa, *Sundlaugarvegur 30a, 105 Reykjavík, T553 0000, www.laugar spa.is*. Saunas, jacuzzis, relaxation rooms, Olympic-sized swimming pool and a gym.

Swimming

See page 64, for information on the country's famous Blue Lagoon; what most people don't know is that within the city there are a number of great geothermal swimming pools for a fraction of the price of the famous one. Entry to them is free if you hold a Reykjavík Welcome Card – and it's only a handful of coins if you don't. Be sure to follow the shower instructions – as the pools aren't heavily treated with chemicals, swimmers are required to wash carefully before entry. Pools are kept at 29°C. Prices in 2015 were ISK 650 for adults, ISK 140 for children.
Laugardalslaug, *Sundlaugarvegur, T411 5100*. The city's largest, with an open-air pool with lanes and slide plus several hot tubs and a sauna. Located in the Laugardalur Valley and sports complex.
Sundhollin, *Baronsstigur, T411 5350*. The oldest pool in the city, this city-centre pool is large and laned and has a couple of hot tubs outside.
Vesturbæjarlaug, *Hofsvallagata, T411 5150*. Outdoor swimming pool with toddler slide and sauna plus hot tubs, just on the outskirts of the city.

Whale watching

Whale-watching trips take place from the old harbour; most offer a free trip if you don't see anything.

Elding Whale Watching, *Ægisgardur 5, T519 5000, www.elding.is*. Whale-watching tours from Reykjavík's old harbour several times a day during summer, once a day in the winter. Also offers puffin-watching tours May-Aug and sea angling May-Sep.
Iceland Excursions, *Harfnarstræti 20, 101 Reykjavík, T540 1313, www.iceland excursions.is*. Whale-watching tours in the Faxafloi Bay plus entry to the Whale Exhibition Centre.
Special Tours, *old harbour, T560 8800, www.lifeofwhalesspecialtours.is*. 3-hr whale-watching tours from Reykjavík.

Whitewater rafting and kayaking

Arctic Rafting, *Laugavegur 11, 101 Reykjavík, T571 2200, www.arcticrafting.is*. Whitewater rafting on the Hvita River 90 mins south of Reykjavík plus a combination of canoeing, quad biking and other adrenalin-filled activities in the same area.

Transport

Air

The country's key international airport is at **Keflavik**, www.kefairport.is, a 50-min drive from Reykjavík (see box, page 18, for transport from the airport to the city). In the city itself, the smaller domestic **Reykjavík Airport**, www.isavia.is, serves destinations around the country including **Akureyri**, the **Westman Islands** and **Húsavík**. There are also flights to **Greenland** and the **Faroe Islands** from this airport. The main airlines, **Eagle Air**, www.eagleair.is, and **Air Iceland**, www.airiceland.is, also offer day tours of Iceland and day trips to Greenland.

Bus

Local Reykjavík's fleet of **Stræto** buses provided a good service around the city but you probably won't need it unless you're staying out of town. If you are staying in the Laugardalur Valley, most hotels run shuttle bus into the city. The bus routes 2, 14, 15, 17 and 19 run between the city centre and Laugardalur Valley.

You can pick up a local bus map from the tourist information centre and if you purchase a Reykjavík Welcome Card, all bus travel in the city is included. A single bus journey costs ISK 400. The city transport website is www.straeto.is.

The 2 key bus terminuses are **Hlemmur**, at the far end of Laugavegur from the centre, and **Laekjartorg**, where the 2 main roads intersect in the centre of the city.

Long distance Reykjavík has 1 long-distance bus terminus, the **BSÍ** bus station, www.bsi.is. It serves Iceland's other key cities and districts but be sure to check availability and routes in advance as routes can be seasonal. A full timetable is available on www.bsi.is. As well as long-distance routes, a regular bus to the **Blue Lagoon** leaves from this bus station and it is possible to book tours to the **Golden Circle** and the **Saga Circle** here.

Car hire

The major international car hire desks are all at Keflavik Airport. Within Reykjavík, car hire can be arranged through most hotels and hostels. Operators include: **Atak**, T554 6040, www.atak.is; **Budget**, T562 6060, www.budget.is; and **Sixt**, T540 2222, www.sixt.is.

Taxi

There are 2 taxi ranks in the centre of Reykjavík, one on Aðalstræti outside the tourist information office and another on Lækjartorg. Taxis are efficient, clean and well run with no need for a tip but are costly. All taxis have meters and fares are charged at standard rates. Expect to pay ISK 20,000 for a 4-km journey. Companies include: **Airport Taxi**, T520 1212, www.airporttaxi.is; **Borgarbílastöðin**, T552 2440, www.borgarbilastodin.is; **BSR Taxis**, T561 0000, www.taxireykjavik.is; or **Hreyfill-Bæjarleiðir**, T588 5522, www.hreyfill.is.

Around
Reykjavík

Many of Iceland's most exciting natural attractions – volcanoes, glaciers and natural hot springs – are accessible from the city in a day trip. Given that the capital has the country's best range of hotels, restaurants and nightlife, most people visiting for a short break will base themselves in the city and travel out each day. It's easy to take a day trip by coach to these places and indeed it's the most convenient and cheapest way to do it. If you want to see them without the crowds or are staying for longer and have a hire car, there are a handful places to stay near these attractions too.

Most long-weekenders to Reykjavík spend half a day in the city and then day trip to the nearby natural attractions. Gulfoss waterfall, Þingvellir National Park and Geysir are the most popular to visit, along with the Blue Lagoon. There are also plenty of activity tours such as hiking, climbing, skidooing, cycling and many more, offering an alternative way to experience the countryside.

Blue Lagoon (Bláa Lonið)
Iceland's top attraction; a thermal pool with an ethereal, other-worldly feel

★Just 40 minutes from the city and a popular stop on the way to or from Keflavík Airport, the Blue Lagoon is one of Iceland's most visited tourist attractions. In a country with such an exuberance of outstanding beauty, this is high praise indeed – especially for what is essentially a lido.

Visitor information 240 Grindavík, T420 8800, www.bluelagoon.com. 1 June-31 August daily 0800-2200, 1 September-31 May daily 1000-2000. June-August adults €45, concessions and children (14-15s) €20, under 14s free; September-May €35, concessions and children (14-15s) €20, under 14s free. Buses run by **Reykjavík Excursions** ⓘ www.re.is, leave several times daily to the Blue Lagoon from the BSÍ bus station or Keflavík Airport, ISK 3600 one way. By car, take Route 41 from Reykjavík towards Keflavík and then Route 43 to Grindavík.

Essential Around Reykjavík

Where to stay

These attractions are most commonly visited in a day trip from the city, but if you want to spend longer than half a day in these spots, there are a few well-located hotels to book, allowing you access to the natural delights without the crowds in the early morning and evening. You can also book cabins in the countryside around the city by visiting the websites www.farmholiday.is, www.volcanohuts.com and www.visiticeland.com.

Restaurants and cafés

Eating out outside the capital is highly variable. Five-star hotels have exemplary restaurants; most hotels have some kind of restaurant, be it homespun and rustic or international in flavor, and if all else fails, try the petrol station. These rest stops usually sell *pylsur*, Icelandic hot dogs, coffee and all manner of snacks and act as informal cafés in areas where the population is so low that there's no need for anything more.

Visiting the lagoon Situated next to the Svartsengi power plant, the Blue Lagoon is a large splash of milky-blue water in the middle of an otherwise desolate volcanic landscape that makes use of the geothermal water passing through the plant. Extra water from the power plant was pumped into the lava fields to drain away but minerals in the water crystallized, thus creating the pool used today. The distinctive hue actually comes from the minerals and blue-green algae that have dissolved into the sea water and which have been proven to have a positive effect on the skin.

The temperature is kept at 36-39°C all year round and gives you a nice fuzzy warm feeling. The bottom of the pool is mainly sand, although at the far corners you'll find some silica mud in pots, especially good for healing skin complaints. Massages and beauty treatments are available at the pool; book in advance. Remember to bring some shampoo, conditioner and moisturiser, as the salt water leaves your skin feeling dry and your hair will be matted if you don't wash it a good few times afterwards. You can hire swimming costumes and towels if you forget to bring them with you. There's also a snack bar and the upmarket **Lava** restaurant that looks out onto the surreal landscape.

Listings Blue Lagoon (Bláa Lonið)

Where to stay

€€€€ Blue Lagoon Clinic and Hotel
240 Grindavík, T420 8800,
www.bluelagoon.com.
15 double rooms and a private lagoon for those being treated at the clinic for skin disorders like psoriasis, and for non-treatment guests. Disabled access. Highly rated for its design with views of moss-clad lava fields. 10-min walk from the Blue Lagoon pool. Local excursions including quad biking and whale watching can be booked through reception.

€€€€ Northern Light Inn
Norðurljósavegur, 1 Northern Lights Rd,
240 Grindavik, T426 8650, www.nli.is.
40 mins from Reykjavík on Route 41.
32 quiet and spacious rooms with geothermal showers and Icelandic down duvets. Free airport and Blue Lagoon transfers and Wi-Fi as well as a restaurant and conference centre. Reservations by email only.

Restaurants

€€€ Lava Restaurant
Blue Lagoon, 240 Grindavik, T420 8800,
www.bluelagoon.com.
This elegant restaurant is an addition to the swimming complex and offers Icelandic ingredients in international combinations – the likes of burgers

and sushi plus beef tenderloin and plenty of high-end wines to go with them. Chefs train by spending time at Michelin star restaurants in London, New York and Paris – this is much more than a post-swimming snack stop. If you prefer something a little lighter after swimming, there's a snack bar and café by the pool.

What to do

Day tours
Several tour operators run trips to the Blue Lagoon, including:
Arctic Adventures, *Laugavegur 11, T562 7000, www.adventures.is.*
Iceland Excursions, *Harfnarstræti 20, 101 Reykjavík, T540 1313, www.grayline.is.*
Reykjavík Excursions, *BSÍ Bus Terminal, 101 Reykjavík, T580 5400, www.re.is.*

Quad bikes
Many quad-biking tours from Reykjavík include the Reykjanes Peninsula, near the Blue Lagoon, on their itineraries.
Iceland Excursions, *Harfnarstræti 20, 101 Reykjavík, T540 1313, www.grayline.is.*
ATV or quad-bike tours on the Reykjanes Peninsula lava fields near the Blue Lagoon and a soothing swim afterwards.

> **Tip...**
> As the route to the airport passes the Blue Lagoon, it's a convenient place to visit before flying home.

Viking World

beautifully designed museum based around a Viking ship

This museum is dedicated to the Vikings and their ships. Located a short distance from Keflavik Airport on the Reykjanes Peninsula, it is in an otherwise unspoilt area next to the sea and surrounded by lava fields, making its modern glass building all the more spectacular. Inside is the exact replica of the Viking ship *Gokstad* from the year AD 870, a boat named *Islendingur*, or *The Icelander*, a ship that actually sailed across the Atlantic to the New York in 2000, along with treasures and context supplied by the Smithsonian. There's also a dramatic representation, Gudridur's Story, telling of what life was like as a woman in the Viking world, and a small Viking village outside.

Visitor information Vikingabraut 1, Njardarvik, Reykjanes Peninsula, T422 2000, www.vikingaheimar.is. May-August daily 1100-1800, September-April daily 1200-1700. ISK 1300, concessions ISK 1000, under 14s free. Take the Keflavik bus or drive.

Visiting the museum What gives this exhibition its real power is Gunnar Marel Eggertsson, the man behind it all. From a family of shipbuilders in the Westman Islands, he traces his lineage back to Norse explorer Leif Eiriksson and had dreamed of building a boat to sail on a transatlantic voyage from a young age. He single-handedly built the Icelander between 1994 and 2006, using drawings from the Viking Ship Museum in Oslo. His dedication and attention to detail makes this a fine celebration of the Viking sailing life and may well change your perceptions of the Viking world.

Golden Circle

popular day trip to some of iceland's natural wonders

The Golden Circle is the highly publicized circular tour of three of Iceland's finest natural and historic features within a day's journey of Reykjavík. Starting at Þingvellir National Park, the ancient site of the Viking parliament, you can then take in Geysir and Strókkur, two spouting geysers, and finish at the highlight, Gullfoss, the Golden Falls, so-named because of the rich rainbow colours you can see as sunlight shines through the mist. The sights are equally worth seeing individually, especially Þingvellir where you could spend a few days walking around the dramatic scenery.

★Þingvellir National Park
49 km northwest of Reykjavík, T482 2660, www.thingvellir.is. Visitor centre and shop daily 0900-1700, free. Restrooms open 24 hrs, ISK 200. Þingvellir Service Centre has information and sells fishing and camping permits. Þingvellir is easily reached by taking Route 1 out of the city towards Mosfellsbær and then Route 36 from which it is signposted. From 24 May to the end of Aug buses to Þingvellir and the Golden Circle go several times daily from the BSÍ bus station, see www.re.is for details. They cost from ISK 9500. It is included on many day tour itineraries.

One of Iceland's most visited sights, Þingvellir (pronounced Thingvellir), is blessed with an active landscape and a remarkable history. Look around as you enter the park and you can see a dramatic rift in the earth, in the shape of dark cliffs rising up from the grassland. This is the American tectonic plate tearing away from the Eurasian plate, moving apart at an average of 2 cm each year. Further across the park you can see the same kind of scar in the opposite hill – the Eurasian plate. What is left in the middle is new land created between the two, neither American nor European.

The same is happening beneath the lake at the centre of Þingvellir. A couple of dive companies can take you underwater to see the air bubbling up at the **Silfra Rift** (see page 71). It's one of the world's most extreme dives and you'll need to wear a dry suit.

The Viking assembly site was at **Lögberg**, or Law Rock, from AD 930 until 1271. From the tourist information centre, take the road down towards the church and small farm building until you reach the car park. The Lögberg is marked with a flag on the right-hand side of the river. It's a natural platform for speeches and the speaker could be seen and heard from some distance around. Anyone attending the assembly had the right to ask for help on any issue from the Law Rock, where discussions began at 1800 on each day of the parliament. All issues were settled in one sitting and generally money changed hands to find a resolution. From here you can look out over the river and Lake Þingvallavatn, with the high wall of the Almannagjá fault, the American plate, behind it. The Öxará River, which flows in and out of the plate towards the lake, was a feature of the Viking parliament. The largest island in the river, **Öxarhólmar**, was the site of many duels, one of the less diplomatic ways of settling a dispute. Adulteresses and female criminals were drowned in a sack filled with heavy stones at the bridge by the church by the Vikings. The water is very cold and it was apparently a quick death.

Soon after Iceland adopted Christianity, around AD 1000, the King of Norway sent timber and a bell for the construction of a **church** at Þingvellir and it has been at the same site ever since, although the current church was rebuilt in 1907. It's beautiful inside with a font that was designed by a local farmer in 1962, and the graveyard contains the graves of two Icelandic poets and some priests of the district.

The other building here, **Þingvallabær**, is a traditional farmhouse built in 1930 for the Alþing millennium celebrations, and now the summer residence of the president of Iceland.

Lake Þingvallavatn is a place where Europe and America come together in terms of wildlife. There are enormous amount of birds here, from the North American great northern diver and Barrow's goldeneye to the European white-tailed eagle. Given that the lake is 83 sq km in surface area and 114 m at its deepest point, with some very big fish, it's not surprising. Four species of arctic char live in the lake as well as brown trout that reputedly weigh up to 30 lb. Their average weight is around 11 lb, so the 30-pounders may be just one of those fisherman's tales. You can fish the lake with a permit from the tourist office.

There are numerous hiking and pony trekking trails throughout Þingvellir. Many trails lead from the Þingvallabær area towards the central **Skógarkot** area, about 2 km away, and then either back to the tourist office or on towards the Eurasian plate at the Hrafnagjárendi Rift. Tourist information centres have maps of the area with marked hiking trails and also sell permits for the campsite. In the summer, park rangers run free hour-long guided walking tours of Þingvellir describing the history and nature of the park leaving at 1000 from the church at Þingvellir.

▸▸ See What to do, page 71.

Geysir

Geysirstofa Museum and visitor centre, T480 6800, www.geysircenter.is. Jan-Apr 1200-1600, May-Aug 1000-1700, Sep-Dec 1200-1600. ISK 1000, under 16s and concessions ISK 800. The outdoor site is free to visit. Regular buses run year round from the BSÍ bus station to Gullfoss and Geysir, see www.re.is. By car from Þingvellir, take Route 36 until you reach Route 35 near the crater at Kerið. Continue until you pass Reykholt and then reach Geysir. From Reykjavík it's quicker to take Routes 1 and 37 south to Hveragerði then turn off onto Route 35 just before Selfoss.

The air is heavy with sulphur, the ground smokes and water streaks high into the air. Geysir is the site of two geysers that spout regularly to the delight of onlookers. By timing your trip early or late in the day you might be able to reclaim the landscape from the coach tours and have it all to yourself.

Icelanders are proud of the fact that Geysir gave its name to all other such hot springs across the world, but today it's a lot less active than it used to be, spouting perhaps four times a day and not as high as the 70-80 m that it used to reach. Strokkur by contrast is so regular you could set your watch by it. Water is forced 25-35 m up into the air by the build-up of steam and the resulting high pressure beneath it every three to five minutes. Make sure you've worked out which way the wind's blowing or you'll get drenched. The active hot springs were noted as far back as 1294 in the sagas and continue to be an impressive sight. Watch the pool of water and as it becomes domed you can tell it's about to blow. On a safety note, the path is clearly marked and you should take care to stick to it. The earth's crust here is very thin in places and small earthquakes can weaken the ground without showing it. Many of the pools of water here are above boiling point so care is needed.

Across the road you'll find the **Geysirstofa Museum** and visitor centre, café, stables, campsite and hotel, all under the same management. This is all part of a multimedia exhibition centre showing how the forces of nature have shaped Iceland into the country it is today, with its waterfalls, volcanoes and glaciers. There's also a small folk museum.

The **Haukadalur Forest** above the geysers is a well-kept secret and a great place to go riding, with wild flowers, waterfalls, fabulous views and barely another person in sight. Ask at the visitor centre about horse-riding tours in the area.

▸▸ See What to do, page 71.

Gullfoss

www.gullfoss.is. Easily reached and clearly marked, take Route 35 from Geysir and you'll reach Gullfoss in about 10 km. Gullfoss is a massive 2-step waterfall on the glacial River Hvítá.

It's a breathtaking expanse of water, beautiful at any time of year and very wet because of the spray no matter what the weather's like. In the early 1900s, Gullfoss was sold to foreign investors who wanted to harness its lucrative hydroelectric power. The local farmer's daughter, Sigríður, was opposed to the scheme and walked 110 km from the farm to Reykjavík several times to protest and enlist lawyers to stop the sale. In 1928 she won the case and at the top of the waterfall there's a monument erected to her memory.

Inside the volcano

Thrihnukagigur Volcano, 20 km from Reykjavík, T863 6640, www.insidethevolcano. com. ISK 39,000. Minimum age limit 12 years. 15 May-30 Sep. Scheduled daily tours include pickup from Reykjavík, leaving at 0800, 1000, 1200 and 1400 (also 1600 Jun-Aug). By car from Reykjavík, follow Sudurlandsvegur road to Route 1. Drive straight for about 15 mins and then turn right onto the Blafjallavegur road, 417. Continue straight until it changes into road 407. Don't turn right onto the gravel part of road 417, continue on road 407 towards the ski resort. After driving for 10 mins after the turn from route 1, you'll see the sign that says "Inside The Volcano – Parking 300 meters".

Iceland is of course famous for its volcanoes and this is its most unique tourist outing: a descent into the dormant **Thrihnukagigur Volcano** in the Blue Mountains. It's an easy day trip and bus transport from the city is also available. After a 50-minute hike up the volcano, you step into a small open cable lift (a little like the type window cleaners use for high-rise buildings) and begin a descent down 120 m to the bottom. Once inside the volcano, it's not hot or sulphurous, but rather like being in a cave with charred walls and multicoloured rock. It's quite something. The tour allows for around 45 minutes in the volcano before the ascent.

You will need hiking boots and warm clothes – the weather in the mountains can be unpredictable and trainers and jeans won't be enough. You need a decent level of fitness to walk up and down the volcano. Fun fact: Tom Cruise has been inside this volcano.

Langjökull Ice Cave

Langjökull Glacier, base camp is at Husafell, 3 hrs by road from Reykjavík, T578 2550, www.icecave.is. ISK 17,900, children 12-15 half price, under 11s free. Tours from base camp 3 times daily Jun-Sep, 2-3 hrs; Oct-May Thu-Sat once daily, 3-4 hrs. Day tours available from Reykjavík can be combined with the Golden Circle.

New in 2015, 7000 sq m of ice has been excavated from underneath Langjökull Glacier to form Europe's largest ice cave. Visitors are transported in 8WD trucks from the edge of the glacier to the mouth of the tunnel where they walk 200 m into the depths of the cave. It's an opportunity to experience Iceland on a whole new sub-glacial level, with blue ice grottos and huge crevasses seen from deep within. Be sure to wear warm clothes and sturdy footwear.

Listings Golden Circle

Where to stay

Þingvellir

€€€ Hotel Ion
Near Þingvellir, T482 3415,
www.ioniceland.is.
This super-styled boutique hotel nestling in the slopes of Mount Hengill just south of Þingvallavatn, has a spa, classy restaurant serving Icelandic specials and a bar made for Northern Lights gazing. Rooms are decorated in ultra-modern Icelandic style.

€€€ Hotel Laxnes
Mosfellsbær, T566 8822,
www.hotellaxnes.is.
This 3-star hotel is 15 mins from Reykjavík in the horse-breeding area of Mosfellsbær, close to Þingvellir. It's a rural hotel with 26 rooms, including studios and family rooms, and offers car rental, activities, day tours and Northern Lights watching.

€ You can camp at Þingvellir 1 Jun-1 Sep. There are 2 camping areas: **Leirar** is adjacent to the service centre (see page 66), while **Vatnskot** is situated at an abandoned farmhouse beside Þingvallavatn Lake at Vatnskot. They are both fairly basic with toilet facilities and you need to buy a permit at the tourist information centre on arrival. Under 13s are free and groups of 10 or more get a 15% discount. See www.thingvellir.is for more information.

Geysir

€€ Hotel Geysir
Haukadal, 801 Selfoss, T480 6800,
www.geysircenter.is.
24 wooden cabins in the wilds of South Iceland with fine views of the geysers and an outdoor thermal pool as well as horse riding, quad biking and Wi-Fi. Unusual and good value with cabins, apartments, double rooms and dormitory accommodation. Price excludes breakfast.

Gullfoss

€€€ Hótel Gullfoss
7 km from Geysir and 3 km from Gulfoss,
T486 8979, www.hotelgullfoss.com.
This small family-run country hotel offers traditional Icelandic food and 16 small and basic rooms. Friendly service and a great view, this is a good hotel for walkers and highland travellers. It has a hot tub on the roof deck, ideal for viewing the Northern Lights in winter.

Restaurants

Þingvellir

€ Þingvellir Café
T482 2660, www.thingvellir.is. Apr-Oct daily 0900-1700; weekends only in winter.
This small café at the national park visitor centre, sells sandwiches, soup and coffee. This is a decent snack stop for walkers but if you're camping at

Þingvellir, you'll want to bring supplies with you.

What to do

Caving
Extreme Iceland, *Vatnagardar 12, 104 Reykjavik, T588 1300, www.extremeiceland.is.* Day tours from Reykjavík to Þingvellir National Park to visit the lava caves and tubes from eruptions that took place about 9000 years ago. Book a trip with this company to walk where the lava once flowed and see the country from the inside out.

Day tours
Arctic Adventures, *Laugavegur 11, T562 7000, www.adventures.is.* Trekking, horse riding, sightseeing, glacier tours, caving, kayaking and hiking.
Iceland Excursions, *Harfnarstræti 20, 101 Reykjavík, T540 1313, www.grayline.is.* Bus tours and activities including Gullfoss and the Golden Circle.
Reykjavík Excursions, *BSÍ Bus Terminal, 101 Reykjavík, T580 5400, www.re.is.* Bus tours and activities including trips to Gullfoss and Geysir.

Diving
Dive.is, *Hólmaslóð 2, 101 Reykjavík, T578 6200, www.dive.is.* Specialist company running diving and snorkelling tours in Iceland, specializing in the Silfra Rift and offering midnight sun snorkelling and diving as well as combination tours with the Blue Lagoon, sightseeing and horse riding.
Iceland Excursions, *Harfnarstræti 20, 101 Reykjavík, T540 1313, www.grayline.is.* A tour company that also offers fissure diving at Silfra and snorkelling.

Hiking
Iceland Like a Local, *Fiskislod 20, 101 Reykjavík, T533 1160, www.iceland-like-a-local.com.* Local tour company offering advice on hikes in the national park as well as trekking and day tours with or without a guide.

Horse riding
Þingvellir was visited by Viking chieftains on horseback once a year for their annual parliament, and it's still a great place to ride. There are 2 designated horse trails through the national park.
Eldhestar, *Völlum, 810 Hveragerði, T480 4800, www.eldhestar.is.*
Ishestar, *Sorlaskeið 26, 220 Hafnarfjördur, T555 7000, www.ishestar.is.* Riding tours of the Golden Circle, Geysir and Gullfoss.
Islenski Hesturinn, *Sturlugata 3, 110 Reykjavík, T434 7979, www.islenski hesturinn.is.* Tours around Þingvellir and the lake.
Laxnes Horse Farm, *Laxnesi 271, Mosfellsbæ, T566 6179, www.laxnes.is.* Various tours including horse riding in Þingvellir and diving in the lake.

Quad bikes
Many quad-biking tours from Reykjavík include the Golden Circle or on their itineraries.
Iceland Excursions, *Harfnarstræti 20, 101 Reykjavík, T540 1313, www.grayline.is.* Off-roading tours and volcano safaris by quad bike or ATV.
Safari Quads, *Lambhagavegur, 113 Reykjavík, T821 1311, www.quad.is.* Tours include New Year's safaris, mountain safaris, night rides and extreme exploration near Mosfellsbaer/Mount Esja. Combined tours with caving, horse riding and snorkelling also available.

Skiing

The Blue Mountains south of Reykjavík are the site for **Inside The Volcano** and also 2 ski complexes. **Bláfjoll** and **Skalafell** are both 25 mins from the city, with ski rental and lessons on weekends. Visit www.skidasvaedi.is for more information.

Snowmobiling

Iceland Excursions, *Harfnarstræti 20, 101 Reykjavík, T540 1313, www.grayline.is.* Offers tours on Langjökull Glacier combined with super jeep tours of the Golden Circle.

Whitewater rafting and kayaking

Most of the activity-based tour operators can organize rafting and kayking.
Arctic Rafting, *Lækjarsel 11, 109 Reykjavík T571 2200, www.arcticrafting.is.* Whitewater rafting on the Hvita River 90 mins south of Reykjavík plus a combination of canoeing, quad biking and other adrenalin-filled activities in the same area.

Around
Iceland

The term 'other-worldly' doesn't do justice to the landscape beyond Reykjavík. Ancient volcanoes, glaciers and hot springs are just some of the things you'll see – people, large towns and traffic are what you won't. It's a mind-blowing place.

It's possible to visit the Snæfesllness Peninsula or South Coast on a long day trip from Reykjavík, but you could spend a week or more exploring them, walking the famous Laugavegur trek or taking the ferry over to the Westman Islands.

Those that venture up to the north are in for a real treat. Iceland's second 'city', Akureyri, has a glorious location on the edge of a deep fjord surrounded by mountains. Nearby, Lake Mývatn is home to some weird and wonderful lava formations, some bathing caves and a huge bird population, and a short drive away is Húsavík, one of the best places in the world for whale watching. From here you can also reach the Arctic Circle and the island of Grímsey. Half of the island sits at 66° north, the only part of the country that's truly arctic. The region is great for walkers, nature lovers and birdwatchers: if you want a break from city life, this is the place to come.

Snæfellsnes Peninsula
dramatic landscape of ice caps and lava fields criss-crossed with hiking trails

★On a clear day you can see the snow-dusted heights of Snæfellsnes across the Faxaflói Bay. It's about 200 km away from the city and can be reached in a day, but staying here for longer allows you to better experience its appeal. The peninsula has a number of small fishing villages, the largest being Stykkishólmur, with a few B&Bs. Snæfellsjökull Glacier itself has a number of claims to fame and snakes down to some strange and beautiful beaches. It's a wonderful place to visit, full of drama and wilderness. Note that there are few restaurants and few hotels in this area so it's wise to book ahead. The nearest big supermarket is at Borgarnes on the Route 54 as you drive to the peninsula, and that to get there you have to drive under Hvalfjörður, a steep and narrow fjord, on is a toll-paying road.

Getting there From Reykjavík take Route 54 north of Borgarnes, Route 56 by Végamot over Kerlingarskarð and then Route 58 to Stykkishólmur. There are daily scheduled buses from Reykjavík's BSI bus station to Stykkishólmur, taking approximately 3½ hours. Visit www.bsi. is or www.sterna.is for up-to-date long-distance bus timetables. Day tours to Snæfellsnes are on offer from many of the Reykjavík tour companies.

Essential Around Iceland

Best place to stay

Hotel Buðir, Snæfellsnes Peninsula, page 77

Finding your feet

Most people hire a car to explore the country, but a decent bus network operates between the main towns from May to September. If you're pushed for time, internal flights are an option with regular connections between Reykjavik and Akureyri, the Westman Islands and Grimsey.

Best places to eat

Hotel Buðir, Snæfellsnes Peninsula, page 78
Hotel Ranga, Hella, page 84
Slippurinn, Haimey, Westman Islands, page 87

The Settlement Centre
Brákarbraut 13-15, 310 Borgarnes, T437 1600, www.landnam.is. Daily 1000-2100. ISK 2500, concessions ISK 1900.

Not strictly on the Snæfellsnes Peninsula, but you'll certainly pass it on the way there. This museum and cultural centre focuses on the Saga and Settlement years and the great Icelandic saga figure, Egil Skallagrimsson. There are audio guides in English and other European languages, and it's all very interesting with multimedia features and downloadable iPhone trails. The story of how the Norwegian Vikings settled Iceland in the late ninth century is one of endurance and extremes, while the Saga tales of Egil are full of drama, bloodshed and the marauding we all more typically associate with the Vikings.

Snæfellsjökull Glacier

Snowmobiling and glacier trips can be taken from the town of Arnarstapi on the southern edge of Snæfellsjökull and other tours from Reykjavík also run to Snæfellsjökull.

This cone-shaped glacier surrounded by a dramatic lavascape was an active volcanic area which last saw eruptions around AD 300 and has recently been turned into a national park. It occupies a special place in Icelandic iconography for a number of reasons. Jules Verne chose it as the location for the start of his *Journey to the Centre of the Earth*, beginning at the small town of Arnarstapi on the south of the peninsula. Nobel prize winning novelist Halldór Laxness also took much of his inspiration from this place, which he described as a meeting of heaven and earth. It's said to be the most powerful energy point in the world, if you believe in new age theories, with a remarkable magical and healing power. And it's also the place where the world's media gathered in the 1990s to witness the first alien landing. It didn't happen, but the hoax was very convincing.

Djúpalónssandur, a beach at the foot of the glacier on Route 574, captures some of the landscape's harsh beauty. There's a small 5-m-deep lagoon to your right as you walk down onto the pebbly beach and a reconstructed turf house which uses driftwood in its structure. Just before you reach it there are four large stones by the side of the track. They are different sizes and unwieldy in shape and are remembered in folktales for their use in classic tests of strength. The heaviest is 154 kg and the lightest 23 kg.

Stykkishólmur

Tourist information is available from Stykkishólmur Campsite, Aðalgata 27, T438 1075, www.stykkisholmur.is.

The small fishing town of Stykkishólmur looks out across Breiðafjörður fjord, a haven for birdlife, seals and the occasional whale. It's the biggest town on the Snæfellsnes Peninsula but the inhabitants are well outnumbered by the wildlife. During the summer months you'll almost certainly see puffins, kittiwakes, guillemots, fulmars and the odd seal around the basalt islands offshore. It's actually impossible to count the number of small islands and skerries in the fjord as the number fluctuates according to the tide. Some of the islands were previously inhabited but nowadays the buildings that remain are only used as summerhouses, if at all. The town itself is affluent with yet an unusual church (as if there are any ordinary churches in this country), a campsite and a handful of guesthouses. There's also a swimming pool with mineral water said to have restorative properties.

From Stykkishólmur, **Seatours** runs boat tours (see page 78) into Breiðafjörður fjord including a birdwatching tour and a trip to **Flatey Island** where most of the buildings date from the 19th century.

Villages around Snæfellsnes

Driving from Stykkishólmur towards Snæfellsjökull on Route 54 there are many scenic views. Just after the small fishing village of **Grundarfjörður**, have a look up

GOING FURTHER

★West Fjords

It's easy to see why most visitors to Iceland bypass the West Fjords. The main road neatly cuts off the peninsula, leaving only the most curious to cross the narrow isthmus that connects it to the mainland. Yet those with the time and inclination to venture off the beaten track are rewarded with some of the most breathtaking scenery Iceland has to offer.

Intense glaciation and a constant battering by Arctic storms have created a landscape unlike the rest of the country. Comprising a third of Iceland's entire coastline, the peninsula is almost entirely mountainous with its dramatic fjords carved into deep craggy inlets, stretching out like fingers into the Denmark Strait.

Travel can be exceptionally slow, as the majority of roads are unpaved and either hug the coast or wind their way through steep mountain passes. A journey of just a few kilometres can take several hours and roads can be closed for months at a time during winter. The communities that live here, in tiny villages nestled into the base of deep fjords, must be self-sufficient and resilient, depending on the sea for their survival.

Despite its isolation, the peninsula supports a population of 7000. The main town, Ísafjörður, is a friendly and surprisingly cosmopolitan place and a good base for arranging activities and trips. Some of Iceland's best hiking is to be found at Hornstrandir, while soaring cliffs like those at Látrabjarg attract millions of breeding sea birds. Mountain biking, fishing and horse trekking are also popular ways to explore the extraordinary landscape with its miles of golden sands, photogenic waterfalls and natural hot springs.

Just 40 minutes by plane from Reykjavik or six hours by car, the peninsula perhaps shouldn't feel as remote as it does. Yet it is a world away from the relatively bright lights of the capital and makes anywhere else in Europe's most sparsely populated nation seem crowded. In a country known for its vast open spaces and rugged beauty, the West Fjords stands out as a true wilderness destination. If it's adventure at the end of the earth that you're looking for, once you cross that isthmus you may never want to leave.

at the mountain before you, **Kirkjufell**, shaped like a church bell and with a huge colony of seabirds living on its steep slopes. Sheep climb up here to graze but it's so steep that it's often impossible to round them up and they have to be shot down. At the foot of the mountain the sand of the beach is grey-white instead of the usual volcanic black, due to the many scallops harvested in the area.

Bjarnarhöfn Shark Museum and Old Church
Bjarnarhöfn, T438 1581, www.bjarnarhofn.is. Daily 0900-1800. ISK 1000.

On the north coast of the peninsula, this small rustic museum is all about the shark-fishing industry and wouldn't be complete without the chance to try some *hakarl*, or rotten shark. It's a curious and quirky little place and an insight into life away from the capital in Iceland, held on the last shark farm in Iceland and hosted by a charming farmer who doesn't speak English. Interesting for adults and kids alike.

Listings Snæfellsnes Peninsula

Where to stay

Staying on this isolated peninsula puts you in touch with what's really special about the Icelandic wilderness. Hotels are basic, apart from the super-luxury, highly priced **Hotel Buðir**.

€€€€ Hotel Buðir
365 Snæfellsnes, T435 6700, www.hotelbudir.is.
This characterful country hotel on the south coast of the peninsula is the best in the area by more than a country mile, if not the entire country. Rooms are somewhat spartan but the setting is incredible, with views over the sandy beach, seals and black wooden church beyond. The hotel's restaurant is one of the best in the whole country.

Stykkishólmur

€€€ Hotel Egilsen
Aðalgata 2, Stykkishólmur, T554 7770, www.egilsen.is.
10-bedroomed boutique hotel in the heart of the town in a lovely historic red building. Quirky and stylish, with

> **Tip…**
> As you leave the capital area, design hotels become fewer and further between and the choice tends to be of small B&Bs and small national chain hotels, with the odd stellar hotel thrown in. If you're on a budget, check out the network of hostels in Iceland at www.hostel.is.

Wi-Fi, power-showers, a home-cooked breakfast and luxurious Coco Mat beds. The best accommodation in town.

€€€ Hotel Stykkishólmur
Borgarbraut 8, T430 2100, www.hringhotels.is.
Modern hotel with fantastic views from its hill-top location. The 100-seat restaurant has a view of Breiðafjörður Bay, and there is free Wi-Fi throughout. Breakfast is a Scandinavian buffet including waffles and a shot of cod liver oil for the brave. It's right next to the town's mineral baths.

€€ Baenir og Braud
Laufásvegur 1, Stykkishólmur, T820 5408, www.baenirogbraud.is.
Small highly regarded B&B in the centre of the town with hot tubs and Wi-Fi, plus a variety of double rooms and spaces for groups and a suite. Cosy and popular.

€€ Hotel Breiðafjördur
Aðalgata 8, Stykkishólmur, T433 2200, www.hotelbreidafjordur.is.
Small family-run hotel in the old part of Stykkishólmur with 11 double rooms, some of which can add an extra bed for families/groups. Internet on site.

€ Grundarfjörður Youth Hostel
Hliðarvegur 15, T895 6533, www.hostel.is. Open May-Sep only.
Great views from this popular corrugated-iron-clad hostel, one of the town's oldest buildings. Also runs boat- and birdwatching tours and you'll need to book in advance in summer.

Private double rooms as well as dorm
beds available.

€ Stykkishólmur Campsite
Aðalgata 27, Stykkishólmur, T438 1075.
The campsite is near the swimming pool
and golf course. Fairly basic, with Wi-Fi,
hot showers, washing machines and
dryers and wardens onsite 0800-2200.

Restaurants

There are not many places to eat out
beyond hotels on the Snæfellsnes
Peninsula. If you are self-catering
or need to buy supplies, the town
of Borgarnes has the closest large
supermarket and is just before you
turn off Route 1 towards the peninsula.

€€€ Hotel Buðir
365 Snæfellsnes, T435 6700,
www.hotelbudir.is.
The hotel's restaurant is open to non-
residents and is one of the very best
in the whole country. Expect creamy
cod soup, Icelandic delicacies including
lamb, seafood and puffin and exquisite
desserts. Expensive but worth the trip
here alone. Great bar too.

€€€ Narfeyrarstofa
Aðalgata 3, 340 Stykkishólmur, T438 1119,
www.narfeyrarstofa.is.
Traditional Icelandic restaurant serving
fish, kelp, mussels, cormorant and shark
as well as burgers.

€€ Fimm Fiskar
Frúarstíg 1, 340 Stykkishólmur, T463 1600,
www.simnet.is/fimmfiskar.
Chalet-style restaurant serving fish – and
in this town, you get the freshest around.

€ Arnabær
Arnastapi, T435 6783, www.snjofell.is/
restaurant. 17 Jun-1 Sep.

> **Tip...**
> Note that outside the capital, it's
> common for restaurants to only open
> for lunch and/or dinner and to close
> by 2100; outside of the peak season
> of June-August most have reduced
> opening hours.

Small restaurant/café in the centre
of Arnastapi on the south coast of
Snæfellsnes serving seafood, meat and
barbecued food as well as home-made
cake and coffee.

What to do

Boat trips and fishing
Seatours, *Smiðustigur 3, Stykkishólmur,*
T433 2254, www.seatours.is. Ferry and
boat company offering tours of the
Breiðafjörður Bay and its many islands.
The half-day tours combining nature
and birdwatching with fresh seafood
gathering are particularly good.
Seatours also operates the Baldur ferry
which takes trips from Stykkishólmur
to the Western Fjords. Also offers sea-
angling tours with nets available from
the harbour.

Day tours
Arctic Adventures, *Laugavegur 11,*
Reykjavík, T562 7000, www.adventures.is.
Day tours including glacier hikes
on Snæfellsjökull.
Iceland Excursions, *Hafnarstraeti 20,*
101 Reykjavík, T540 1313, www.grayline.is.
Day tours and hiking trips to the
south coast and bus tours of the
Snæfellsnes Peninsula.
Reykjavík Excursions, *BSÍ bus station,*
101 Reykjavík, T580 5400, www.re.is.
Day tours running to Jökulsárlón,
Snæfellsnes Peninsula and Thorsmork.

Glacier tours and snowmobiling

Snjofell, *Arnastapi, Snæfellsnes, T435 6783, www.snjofell.is.* Snowmobile and snow cat tours of Snæfellsjökull glacier from the town of Arnastapi on the south coast of Snæfellsnes, plus guided drives on to the snow. Scheduled tours take place Mar-Sep 6 times daily from 1000.

Horse riding

Extreme Iceland, *Vatnagarðar 12, 104 Reykjavík, T588 1300, www.extreme iceland.is. Jun-Sep.* Tour company running day-long horse riding tours of Snæfellsnes Peninsula from Keflavik airport, perfect for stopovers.
Hotel Buðir, *365 Snæfellsnes, T435 6700, www.hotelbudir.is.* With stables nearby,

Hotel Buðir can arrange 1-day and half-day horse riding tours along the south of the peninsula.

Swimming
Stykkishólmur Mineral Baths,

Borgarbraut 4, 340 Stykkishólmur, T433 8150, sundlaug@stykkisholmur.is. Outdoor and indoor municipal swimming pool with mineral-rich water said to have restorative benefits. Baby pool, adult pool, slide and hot tubs.

Transport

Bus
See www.straeto.is or www.bsi.is for details on routes to Snæfellsnes Peninsula.

Landmannalaugar
long-distance hiking trail across some of Iceland's best geothermal landscapes

★Landmannalaugar (pronounced Lant-manna-lawyer) in the central highlands is one of Iceland's beauty spots. It's an area of recent volcanic activity with huge rhyolite mountains stained sulphurous yellow and sandstone orange backing onto fields of shining obsidian chunks and rugged lava. You can relax naked in the hot mountain stream and pool in the midst of these beautiful surroundings or hike through dramatic landscapes on the four-day 'Laugavegurinn to the forest of Þorsmörk' trek. If you want to stay longer, there's a hut at Landmannalaugar and you can camp but be aware that there are no shops in the area at all. All the main tour companies run tours here via the odd volcano or natural wonder on the way. You can combine it with a visit to Hekla, a fierce volcano that used to be known as the 'mouth of hell'.

Getting there The easiest way to reach the area is to drive, but make sure your car is up to it. Ideally you need a 4WD as you may have to cross a few rivers on the way. A bus runs June to mid-September from the BSÍ bus station daily at 0830 costing ISK 9000 each way – convenient for the Laugavegurinn (see below) or a brief day trip of 1¾ hours.

Laugavegurinn (Laugavegur Hiking Trail)
www.landmannalaugar.info.

Also here also is Laugavegurinn, the most famous of Iceland's hikes, a four-day walk linking Landmannalaugar and the forest of Þorsmörk to the south. From

Landmannalaugar to Þorsmörk the landscape drops 600 m and you have some fantastic views of the glaciers in the area, Mýrðalsjökull, Eyjafjallajökull and Tindfjallajökull, as well as the rhyolite mountains, gorges and geothermal springs. You also have the nerve-testing challenge of a few mountain rivers to cross. It's a route that can easily be done independently, but you can also have it all arranged for you by one of the tour companies.

A very useful pocket-sized book *The Laugavegur Hiking Trail*, by Leifur Þorsteinsson and Guðjón Magnússon, provides practical information on distances and equipment, as well as some basic maps and brief descriptions of the surroundings.

Listings Landmannalaugar

Where to stay

It's possible to stay at the hot springs, but book as far ahead as possible. If you're planning to do the Laugavegurinn hike, you will need to book hiking hut accommodation ahead of time and plan your trip properly. Contact **The Icelandic Hiking Association**, www.fi.is, to book huts en route and at the site.

€ Skáli Fí
T568 2533, www.fi.is. 1 Jul-30 Sep.
Run by the Icelandic Hiking Association, this basic wooden hut at Landmannalaugar has 75 beds (bring a sleeping bag) in dorm rooms and a campsite, kitchen and decent bathroom facilities. Offers horse riding and a perfect location beside the natural hot pool.

Restaurants

€ Skáli Fí
Landmannalaugar, T568 2533, www.fi.is.
Snacks, hot dogs, hot chocolate and sandwiches. Very simple snack stop with a small supermarket with supplies for campers.

What to do

Day tours
Iceland Excursions, *Hafnarstraeti 20, 101 Reykjavík, T540 1313, www.grayline.is.* Day tours and hiking trips as well as super-jeep trips to Thorsmörk Forest, south of Landmannalaugar.
Mountain Taxi, *Skeiðarás 10, 210 Garðabær, T544 5252, www.mountaintaxi.is.* Superjeep tours from Reykjavík that take you straight to Landmannalaugar via extraordinary scenery.

Hiking
Arctic Adventures, *Laugavegur 11, 101 Reykjavík, T562 7000, www.adventures.is.* Guided hiking around the Thorsmork/Landmannalaugar region and south Iceland in general.
Ferðafelag Islands, *Mörkin 6, T568 2535, www.fi.is.* The Icelandic Touring Association offers guided hiking tours, including to Landmannalaugar, led by experienced non-professional guides. You have to provide your own equipment and food. They also run the country's network of hiking huts.

Horse riding

Shorter horse-riding tours of Landmannalaugar itself are available in Jul and Aug with **Hraun Hestar** (Rauðalæk, T566 6693, www.hnakkur.com).

Eldhestar, *Vollum, 810 Hveragerði, T480 4800, www.eldhestar.is*. Day and longer tours around south Iceland including multi-day tours to Landmannalaugar.

Hekluhestar, *Austvaðsholt, 851 Hella, South Iceland, T487 6598, www.hekluhestar.is*. 6- and 8-day tours into the highlands and Landmannalaugar plus day tours and summer night horse trekking.

Ishestar, *Sorlaskeið 26, 220 Hafnarfjorður, T555 7000, www.ishestar.is*. 8-day horse riding treks around Hekla and Landmannalaugar from a base near Reykjavík.

Transport

Bus

See www.straeto.is or www.bsi.is for details on routes to Landmannalaugar.

South Coast

charming villages, a stunning lagoon and Iceland's most infamous volcano

Driving south from Reykjavík, the countryside turns rural with gentle rolling hills and sudden dramatic volcanoes. It is in this area that Eyafjallajökull erupted in 2010, sending up a plume of ash that made air travel dangerous and stopped flights from around the world. It's not the only dangerous volcano in these parts, but it's one that you can get up close to now, on various hiking trails. The most notable visitor attraction in south Iceland is the acclaimed glacial lagoon Jökulsárlón, which has starred in many films and TV shows and is unbelievably beautiful. You can't realistically reach it in a day from Reykjavík, but with a stop in south Iceland overnight, it can be done in a short stay in the country.

Mount Hengill Geothermal Springs

Reykjadalur, Hveragerði. Guided trips to the area are available from Reykjavík through Arctic Adventures, www.adventures.is.

The town of **Hveragerði**, 40 km east of Reykjavík in south Iceland is known for its hot springs and has a series of greenhouses making the most of the warmer conditions to grow flowers, fruit and vegetables. It's an active volcanic zone and when an earthquake hit a few years ago it created a series of geothermal pools, the best of which are between Reykjadalur and Mount Hengill. It takes about three hours to reach them on foot from Hveragerði. When you get there you'll find a natural hot bath and small streams along the valley side.

Eyafjallajökull Erupts Visitor Centre

Þorvaldseyri, 861 Hvolsvöllur, T487 5757, www.icelanderupts.is. May daily 1000-1600, Jun-Aug daily 0900-1800, Sep daily 1000-1600, Oct-Apr daily 1100-1600. ISK 800, under 12s free. The centre is on Route 1 about 140 km from Reykjavík and about 40 km from Hvolsvöllur. The building is on the south side of the motorway, 250 m east of Þorvaldseyri Farm.

ON THE ROAD

As seen on screen

Iceland is a fantastic place to make a film – there's the light that means in summer you can shoot for nearly 23 hours without stopping, the other-worldly landscapes that don't have to be dressed to look like an alien environment or post-apocalyptic wasteland, and, oh yes, some hefty subsidies to help you finance your work too. If you want to jet set around the country and view the remarkable scenes you've seen in some of these films, here's where to start.

Fortitude (2015)

A British psychological thriller television drama starring Michael Gambon and Christopher Eccleston set in the Arctic town of Fortitude. Filmed in the villages of Eskifjörður and Reyðarfjörður in Iceland's East Fjords, a second series has already been planned.

Noah (2014)

This film, starring Russell Crowe, all about the biblical Noah, uses Reynisfjara Beach, in south Iceland, and Fossvogur in Reykjavík as backdrops for the apocalyptic deluge.

Oblivion (2013)

This Tom Cruise action film is set in the future, where the lead character Jack Harper is sent back to Earth to extract its remaining resources. In real life, the largely uninhabited area around Jarlhettur Mountain, northeast of Þingvellir National Park, plays the role of a desolate landscape to perfection.

This visitor centre was set up by an enterprising farmer in the wake of the 2010 Eyafjallajökull eruption, which stopped air traffic across the world, in response to the number of people who visited his farm to find out about the impact of it on their lives. Inside you'll find an exhibition, short film and photography on the event, all hosted by the family most affected by the eruption. You can see the volcano from this small farm and get a real sense of how it looms over the people living in this area.

★ Jökulsárlón Glacial Lagoon

Uppsölom 1, 781 Höfn, www.jokulsarlon.com. Located between Hofn and Skaftafell, around 4½ hrs or 377 km from Reykjavík. Follow Route 1 southeast until you see it.

This stunning glacial lagoon in the far southeast of Iceland isn't accessible from Reykjavík in a day but the extra day or two spent in this part of the country is well worth it. The lagoon is full of floating icebergs rimmed with black sand with volcanic mountains in the background. It's like nothing you've ever seen before –

The Secret Life of Walter Mitty (2013)

It's not all alien landscapes and barren war scenes though: the Ben Stiller comedy *The Secret Life of Walter Mitty* was also filmed in Iceland, an adventure comedy drama where a timid photo editor goes on a once-in-a-lifetime adventure. Much of the filming was done around Seyðisfjörður in East Iceland, and Stykkisholmur on the Snæfellsjökull Peninsula also featured.

Prometheus (2012)

This Ridley Scott film, the prequel to *Alien*, used Dettifoss, a huge waterfall in Vatnajökull National Park, in its opening scenes, and the land around Hekla, a volcano in southern Iceland, to conjure up an alien world.

Game of Thrones (2011-2015)

This HBO TV series about seven noble families fighting for their kingdoms has the wastelands of the Land Beyond The Wall and the Wildlings threatening to upend it into chaos underlying it all. This land, a barren snowy wilderness, is an area around Lake Mývatn in North Iceland, filmed in winter.

Flags Of Our Fathers (2006)

Clint Eastwood directed this film about the six men who raised the flag at the Battle of Iwo Jima, a turning point in the Second World War. He used an area of the Reykjanes Peninsula, close to the airport, to replicated the black sands of Iwo Jima.

Batman Begins (2005)

Christopher Nolan's epic *Batman* prequel was shot in a number of locations around Iceland, including the dramatic scenery of Skaftafell National Park and Sveinfellsjökull in Vatnajökull National Park, which stood in for Bhutan where Christian Bale did his ninja training.

unless you've seen *Die Another Day*, *Lara Croft Tomb Raider*, *Batman Begins* and a good number of other action movies for which it has provided a backdrop. Bordering **Vatnajökull (Skaftafell) National Park**, the lagoon was created when the glacier beyond it started to retreat inland. It is the deepest lake in Iceland and is considered one of its natural wonders. Explore it by boat or snowmobile around the edge, from where you can see the pale blue icebergs floating in the lake. Whatever you do, don't forget a camera. The nearby tongue of the Breiðamerkurjökull **Glacier** is also major attraction for tourists, and you can take snowmobile and jeep tours to the glacier, which include visits to the glacial lagoon.

Where to stay

There is nowhere to stay directly next to the glacial lagoon, but these hotels are well placed if you're planning to visit and stay somewhere close by. Vík is about halfway between Reykjavík and Jökulsárlón.

€€€€-€€€ Hotel Ranga
Sudurlandsvegur, 851 Hella, T487 5700, www.hotelranga.is.
South Iceland's premier hotel is this 4-star cabin-style building with numerous quirks and qualities. It's well placed for visiting Jökulsárlón (you can reach it easily in a day trip from here). Steep yourself in a hot tub under the Northern Lights; book one of its extravagant continent-themed suites, or stay in more rustic country-style accommodation on the ground floor. The restaurant serves up an array of delicious but highly unlikely grub – crocodile, puffin, kangaroo – and the hotel's Scandinavian breakfast is one of the best in the country.

€€ Guesthouse Vellir
Myrdal near Vik, T570 2700, www.farmholidays.is.
This small country B&B is 19 km east of Vik and has 3 double rooms and 4 triple rooms with en suite plus 4 double rooms with shared facilities. They can arrange horse riding and have sheep, horses, rabbits, dogs and ducks on their farm.

€€ Volcano Hotel
Ketilsstaðaskóli, 871 Vík, T486 1200, www.volcanohotel.is.
Small modern B&B 12 km west of the town of Vík on the south coast surrounded by volcanic mountains and black sand beaches. 7 rooms, including 4 family rooms. Serves breakfast and dinner only.

€ Vik Youth Hostel
Sudurvikurvegur 5, Vik, T487 1106, www.hostel.is.
Small youth hostel with Wi-Fi, kitchen and dining room, with family rooms, dorms and a shop.

Restaurants

€€€ Hotel Ranga
Sudurlandsvegur, 851 Hella, T487 5700, www.hotelranga.is.
Absolutely worth the trip outside the capital, this restaurant in south Iceland overlooks a salmon river and has salmon, lobster soup, reindeer and chicken on the menu. It's a high-end spot in an unusual location.

What to do

Boat trips

Ice Lagoon, *Sunnuhlíð, 781 Hornafjörður, T860 9996, www.icelagoon.com. 1 May-31 Aug.* Zodiac boat tours of Jökulsárlón with private tours, adventure tours and evening tours.

Day tours

Arctic Adventures, *Laugavegur 11, Reykjavík, T562 7000, www.adventures.is.* Day tours of southern Iceland and hot spring hikes.
Arctic Rafting, *Laugarvegur 11, 101 Reykjavík, T571 2200, www.arcticrafting.com.* Reykjavík-based tour company running day-long rafting tours in fast running rivers in South Iceland.

Iceland Excursions, *Hafnarstraeti 20, 101 Reykjavík, T540 1313, www.grayline.is.* Day tours and hiking trips to the south coast and Jökulsárlón.

Reykjavík Excursions, *BSÍ bus station, 101 Reykjavík, T580 5400, www.re.is.* Day tours to Jökulsárlón.

Snowmobiling

Arcanum Adventures, *Ytri Solheimar 1, 871 Vk Mýrdal, T487 1500, www.arcanum.is.* Adventure tour company offering snowmobiling on Myrðalsjökull glacier.

Iceland Eskimos, *Skutuvogur 1b, 104 Reykjavik, T414 1500, www.iceland. eskimos.is.* Tour operator organizing day tours and snowmobiling around the Jökulsárlón area.

Transport

Air

Westman Islands Airline has flights to the **Westman Islands** from the south coast town of Bakki, taking 5 mins.

Bus

See www.straeto.is or www.bsi.is for details on routes to South Iceland.

Ferry

Ferries to the **Westman Islands** sail from Landeyjahöfn and Þorlákshöfn several times daily, see www.herjolfur.is or call T481 2800 for details. See also page 88.

Vestmannaeyjar (Westman Islands)

volcanic archipelago known for its puffins, outdoor festival and unusual golf course

This archipelago of 15 islands and 30 smaller skerries just off the south coast of Iceland was created by submarine volcanic eruptions. The only inhabited island of the group is Heimaey, which covers an area of just over 13 sq km with steep cliffs and two volcanoes. There's an airport on Heimaey but the islands are accessible by ferry.

Heimaey

There are several museums on Heimaey, the most interesting of which is the **Eldheimar Museum** ⓘ *Gerðisbraut 10, T488 2000, www.eldheimar.is, mid-Apr to mid-Oct daily 1100-1800, mid-Oct to mid-Apr daily 1300-1700, ISK 2300, children aged 10-18 ISK1200, under 10s free.* The interactive exhibition focuses on Iceland's biggest natural disaster, the 1973 volcanic eruption in Vestmannaeyjar, which nearly destroyed the whole town and saw the evacuation of the entire population.

Also worth a look are the **Sæheimar Aquarium and Natural History Museum** ⓘ *Heiðarvegur 12, T481 1997, www.saeheimar.is, ISK 1000, children free; mid-May to mid-Sep daily 1100-1700; mid-Sep to mid-May Sat 1300-1600,* where you might see injured puffins being cared for at the bird hospital, and the **Sagnheimar Folk Museum** ⓘ *T488 2045, www.sagnheimar.is, ISK 1000, under 18s free.*

Locally Heimaey is best known for its wild annual festival, Þjóðhátíð, in August when up to 10,000 people descend on the island to party, recovering the next day to catch baby puffins and send them out to sea until they get bigger. It's quite a sight and isn't just related to the festival – come any time in August to see the children of the Westman Islands collect young, hungry puffins who have tottered from their burrows towards the bright lights of the town. Children roam the streets, carefully picking the puffins up in cardboard boxes to take them home for the night and then return them to nature in the morning, throwing them high from the cliff tops to places where they can survive and thrive.

As well as this unique summer event, the island has a **golf course** (see What to do, below) with high repute where you can play under the midnight sun in June and July and watch puffins as you sink puts in an unusual lava-based course with views of the Atlantic. **Hiking** is the other main attraction here, with two volcanoes and plenty of terrain to cover as well as plentiful bird life. **Birdwatchers** will enjoy walking the coastal paths along the cliffs where you can see manx shearwater, storm petral, leach petral, passerine and waders.

Eldfell and Helgafell volcanoes
The tourist information centre has a number of free maps with walking trails marked on them. The walk up Eldfell, 'fire mountain', takes about 30 mins.

Both of these volcanoes stand at 226 m high and are within easy walking distance of the town centre. You really need walking boots as the trail over lava is a little craggy at times. From the top of Eldfell you can see how the crater imploded on itself. Some parts of the ground are still slightly warm.

Listings Vestmannaeyjar (Westman Islands)

Where to stay

Accommodation on the Westman Isles is cheap and cheerful – designer hotels have yet to make an appearance. Book well in advance if you plan to visit in Aug.

€€ Guesthouse Árný
Illugata 7, 900 Vestmannaeyjar, T899 2582, www.arny.is.
Up the hill from the harbour towards the swimming pool and airport, a homely guesthouse with dorms, single and double rooms, and washing and cooking facilities. Cheaper sleeping-bag accommodation also available.

€€ Guesthouse Hreiðrið
Faxastígur 33, 900 Vestmannaeyjar, T481 1045, http://tourist.eyjar.is.

Private rooms, sleeping-bag accommodation and kitchen facilities available in this small, central guesthouse made from 2 adjoining hotels in the town centre.

€€ Hotel Eyjar
Barustigur 2, 900 Vestmannaeyjar, T481 3636, www.hoteleyjar.is.
10 1- and 2-person apartments with shower, kitchenette, TV and Wi-Fi in the centre of town with a daily breakfast buffet.

€€ Hotel Vestmannaeyjar
Vestmannabraut 29, T481 2900, www.hotelvestmannaeyjar.is.
3-star hotel with 21 rooms plus a seafood restaurant, sauna and hot tubs. Some triple rooms. Clean and basic Scandinavian design.

€ Campsite
Herjólfsdalur, 900 Vestmannaeyjar, T864 4998, www.vestmannaeyjar.is.
Small camping area beside the golf course and cliffs where puffins burrow in the summer. Basic facilities consisting of a bathroom and a hut for shelter. In the heart of the action during the island's annual festival.

€ Hostel Vestmannaeyjar
Sunnuholl, Vestmannabraut 28, T481 2900, www.hostel.is.
24 beds in this hostel including double rooms, triples and shared rooms for 4 and 5. Kitchen, common room, café and internet.

Restaurants

€€ Einsi Kaldi
Vestmannabraut 28, T481 1415, www.einsikaldi.is.
Smart, upmarket restaurant serving lobster, fish and local specials.

€€ Slippurinn
Strandvegur 76, T481 1515, http://slippurinn.com.
Trendy pared back interior and Icelandic dishes. Best place to eat on Heimaey.

€ 900 Grillhus/Topp Pizza
Vestmannabraut 23, T482 1000.
Burgers, pizza and fish and chips, Icelandic style. Popular with anyone wanting a fast food fix.

Festivals

Jun Westman Islands **Open Amateau** golf competition that takes place on the Vestmannaeyjar Golf Course over 2 days at the start of Jun.
1st weekend in Aug **Summer Bank Holiday/Þjóðhátíð** Celebrating the traditional shopkeepers' break, this bank holiday is celebrated with wild parties, particularly on the Westman Islands, which host the wildest Icelandic party of the year. You should book well in advance if you plan to visit.

What to do

Boat trips and fishing
Viking Tours, *Tangagötu 7, 900 Vestmannaeyjar, T488 4884, www.vikingtours.is.* Tours around the islands, in search of whales or to the newest island in the world, the volcanic island of Surtsey, which appeared in the 1960s. Deep-sea fishing tours available on request.

Golf
Golf is a popular sport in Iceland. The key difference between playing at home and playing here is that you'll be playing on a lava field with potentially unpredictable winds, and could play under the midnight sun at any time of day or night in the summer.
Westman Islands Golf Club (Golfklúbbur Vestmannaeyjar), *PO Box 168, Heimaey, 902 Vestmannaeyjar, T481 2363, www.gvgolf.is.* Iceland's best golf course and one of the most unusual in the world, set in an old volcano by the Atlantic, next to nesting puffins. The annual **Volcano Open** takes place here in Jun (see Festivals). Wind directions can be challenging. In the evening when everyone has played their round, snacks of puffin and flatbread are handed out.

Whale watching
Viking Tours, *Tangagötu 7, 900 Vestmannaeyjar, T488 4884, www.vikingtours.is.* 1- to 2-hr tours around the Westman Islands where the highest density of Orca are found.

Transport

For further travel information see www.visitwestmanislands.com.

Air

There is an airport on the Westman Islands. **Air Iceland** (www.airiceland.is) and **Eagle Air**, www.eagleair.is, offer scheduled flights from **Reykjavík**, taking 20 mins.

Ferry

The **Herjólfur Ferry**, T481 2800, www.herjolfur.is, sails to Heimaey on the Westman Islands several times daily. Ferries leave from 2 harbours on the mainland: **Þorlákshöfn** (1 hr by bus from Reykjavík BSÍ bus station), 3 hrs, ISK 3360; and from **Landeyjahofn** (2 hrs by bus from Reykjavík BSÍ bus station), 30 mins, ISK 1260. For precise details on timetables and fares, see www.bsi.is. Ferries may be cancelled due to bad weather, especially in winter. The ferry runs more frequently at the beginning of Aug for the festival (see page 87), but is often fully booked at this time, so be sure to book in advance if planning to visit the festival.

Akureyri

relaxed town with good facilities; a base for exploring the north

Akureyri is the country's second-largest city, although small town is a more appropriate description, located in a peaceful area on the edge of a deep fjord surrounded by mountains. The fresh air and mountains lend the town a relaxing alpine quality. Only 45 minutes on a plane from Reykjavík, Akureyri is almost a full day's drive from the city and if you're in Iceland for a week it's well worth the effort of getting here. This is what the majority of the country is like – isolated and surrounded by unrestricted natural and geological wonders.

The old town of Akureyri extends from the tourist information centre towards the airport. It's a random collection of corrugated-iron housing, some dating back to when the Danish settled the town, and makes for a pleasant walk despite being mainly residential.

Essential Akureyri

Getting around

Akureyri is compact enough to explore on foot although to get to neighbouring towns and hiking areas a car is invaluable. Local buses run frequently enough to let you take a day trip to other towns; during the winter it's a bit more difficult. The city buses are free.

Akureyri Art Museum
Kaupvangsstræti 12, 600 Akureyri, T461 2610, www.listak.is. Tue-Sun 1200-1700. Free.

One of the youngest art museums in Iceland, Akureyri Art Museum displays modern Icelandic art, especially local art, and a variety of international touring exhibitions including collaborations with Lapland and Greenland. Special attention is paid to participation with locals and visitors. Kaupvangsstræti is known as the art canyon and is the centre of the artistic movement in Akureyri, known locally as 'arts alley'. You'll also find the Akureyri School of Visual Arts, artists' studios, small commercial galleries and guest studios for visiting artists on this street.

Akureyri Museum

Aðalstræti 58, 600 Akureyri, T462 4162, www.minjasafnid.is. 1 Jun-15 Sep daily 1000-1700, 16 Sep-31 May Sat 1400-1600 and by arrangement. ISK 1000, under 18s free; day pass for entry into 5 museums ISK 2000.

This small historical museum in the old town tracing the settlement of the Eyjafjörður district and the town of Akureyri. It displays anything from family life, fishing and settlement, heathen burial customs and historic photography, all of which looks back to a simpler and harder way of living. There are two permanent exhibitions, one depicting Eyjafjörður from early times and the other looking at Akureyri, the town on the bay. All the exhibition texts are in English; the museum garden is a good picnic spot.

Akureyri Botanical Gardens

Eyrarlandsvegur, 600 Akureyri, T462 7487, www.lystigardur.akureyri.is. Jun-Sep Mon-Fri 0800-2200, Sat-Sun 0900-2200.

The gardens were opened by a group of ladies in 1912 and are the world's northernmost botanical gardens. The public gardens have botanical specimens from Iceland as well as imported flowers, trees and shrubs. The hills and dales around Akureyri, Mývatn and Húsavík contain some of the oldest forests remaining in Iceland, although many of them are less than 2 m high. The gardens are very peaceful and worth visiting in good weather.

Kjarnaskógur Forest

Kjarnaskógur, 600 Akureyri, T462 4047, www.kjarnaskogur.is.

Kjarnaskógur Forest is Iceland's most visited forest with more than a million trees plus hiking and mountain biking trails. Just inside the town towards the airport, you can walk along streams and larch trees and take in the views of Eyjafjörður fjord. You can still see the remains of old peasant farms amid the trees too and there is a birdwatching shelter by the Hundatjorn marsh at Naustaborgir. In winter the area is prepared for cross-country skiing; contact the cross country trails phone for more information, T878 4050.

Nonni's House (Nonnahús)

Aðalstræti 54, 600 Akureyri, T462 3555, www.nonni.is. 1 Jun-1 Sep daily 1000-1700, otherwise by arrangement. ISK 900, under 17s free.

This wooden building next to the Akureyri Museum is the childhood home of the children's author Nonni, the Reverend Jón Sveinsson, dating from the mid-1800s. He's primarily known in Germany and France for his children's stories. The house is one of the oldest in the city.

The Christmas Garden (Jólagarðurinn)
Eyjafjarðarsveit, 601 Akureyri, T463 1433, jolagard@simnet.is. Jun-Aug 1000-2100, Sep-Dec 1400-2100, Jan-May 1400-1800.

If you've always wanted to know how the Icelandic tradition about the 13 yuletide lads started or want to know more about other Icelandic folk traditions surrounding Christmas, this is the place to come. This small café/shop/museum specializing in all things Yuletide is past the airport south of Akureyri. The café serves traditional food too, including cakes and *hangikjöt* (smoked lamb).

Listings Akureyri

Tourist information

Tourist information centre
*Strandgata 12, T450 1050,
www.visitakureyri.is.*
The website www.visitakureyri.is is also a useful source of information.

Where to stay

Akureyri has a wide array of places to stay. The website for north Iceland, www.northiceland.is, has a comprehensive listing of all the hotels, B&Bs, campsites and hostels in the area.

€€ Hotel Akureyri
Hafnarstræti 67, 600 Akureyri, T462 5600, www.hotelakureyri.is.
Harbourside apartment hotel with views of the mountains. 4 apartments with 2-3 bedrooms. Kitchenette, living room and bathroom. Breakfast provided. Good for families.

€€ Hótel Edda Akureyri
Akureyri v/Þorunnarstræti, 600 Akureyri, T444 4000, www.hoteledda.is.
Modern hotel in the centre of the town with 200 rooms. Restaurant, bar and outdoor barbecue when the weather is nice.

€€ Hótel Kea
Hafnarstræti 87-89, 600 Akureyri, T460 2000, www.keahotels.is.
Large, smart, modern hotel in the heart of Akureyri. Free Wi-Fi plus discounted access to a nearby gym and spa.

€€ Hotel Nordurland
Geislagata 7, 600 Akureyri, T462 2600, www.keahotels.is.
Small central hotel with access to gym and spa and Wi-Fi throughout.

€€ Icelandair Hotel Akureyri
Thingvallastraeti 23, Akureyri, T518 1000, www.icelandairhotels.com.
The town's newest hotel is a friendly modern place with 100 rooms close to the town's swimming pool. The most stylish place to stay, a short walk from the centre.

€ Akureyri Youth Hostel
Stórholt 1, 603 Akureyri, T462 3657, www.hostel.is.
A 15-min walk out of the city, the family that runs this small hostel is really friendly. Dorms, single and double rooms plus 2 summerhouses and a cabin. They also run tours and can help arrange skiing and day tours to Greenland and around the north of Iceland in the summer.

€ Centrum Hostel
Hafnarstraeti 102, Akureyri, T892 9838,
www.centrumhostel.is.
7 dorm rooms plus family rooms, single
and double rooms. Central location so in
that regard better than the youth hostel
(below) if you don't have your own
transport. Kitchen, lounge and TV.

€ Húsabrekka Campsite
across the fjord from Akureyri on the
eastern shore of Eyjafjörður, T462 4921.
Basic campsite with wonderful views,
close to the road, about 6 km from
Akureyri with caravan, cabin and
camping accommodation.

Festivals

26-29 Jun **The Arctic Open** Annual
golf tournament held in the midnight
sun at Akureyri Golf Club, a 4-day
international event for amateurs
and professionals.

What to do

Bike hire
There is a mountain bike trail at
Kjarnaskogur Forest and the town is a
good place to cycle around. Bikes can be
hired from **The Viking**, Hafnarstraeti 104,
Akureyri, www.theviking.is.

Day tours
Saga Travel, *Kaupvangsstraeti 4, 602*
Akureyri, T558 8888, www.sagatravel.is.
Day tours from Akureyri to Mývatn,
Dettifoss, Goðafoss, Húsavík and more.
Private tours and super-jeep tours available.
SBA-Norðurleið, *Hjalteyragata 10,*
600 Akureyri, T550 0700, www.sba.is.
Day tours from Akureyri by bus including
Lake Mývatn, Goðafoss waterfall,
Dettifoss waterfall, whale watching
in Húsavík and the Asbirgi.

Golf
Akureyri Golf Club, *600 Akureyri, T462*
2974, www.gagolf.is, www.arcticopen.is.
Host of the Arctic Open (late Jun)
offering games of midnight golf.

Heliskiing
Arctic Heliskiing, *620 Dalvik, T858 3000,*
www.arcticheliskiing.com. Adventure
heliskiing company offering tours in North
Iceland and Greenland. 4- and 6-day
programmes starting from Akureyri.

Horse riding
Katúr, *Vikurgil 13, Akureyri, T695 7218,*
www.hestaleiga.is. 1-, 2- and 3-hr
horseback tours from a base 5 mins
from the centre of town.
Polar Hestur, *Grytubakki11, 601 Akureyri,*
T463 3179, www.polarhestar.is. Stables
offering horse-riding trips along the
remote valleys of Eyjafjörður, often
accompanied by herds of free running
Icelandic ponies. Transport from Akureyri
can be arranged.
Skjaldarvík, *Skjaldarvík, 601 Akureyri,*
T552 5200, www.skjaldarvik.is. Short tours
and night trips in the Skjaldarvik area,
just outside Akureyri. Pick-up possible;
soak in their hot tub after your trip.

Quad bikes
Saga Travel, *Kaupvangsstraeti 4, 602*
Akureyri, T558 8888, www.sagatravel.is.
1-hr quad-bike tours of the Öxnadalur,
near Akureyri.

Skiing
Hliðarfjall, *Akureyrarbær, T462 2280,*
www.hlidarfjall.is. Opening hours are
variable through the season. Hliðarfjall
is the key skiing mountain just outside
Akureyri. It has a ski school and ski rental.

Swimming

Akureyri Thermal Pool, *Þingvallastræti 21, 600 Akureyri, T461 4455, www.visit akureyri.is. Open year round.* 2 outdoor pools, 4 hot tubs, sauna, steam room, jets, water slides and an indoor pool, all geothermally heated.

Whale watching

Arctic Sea Tours, *Dalvik Harbour, Eyjafjordur, T771 7600, www.arctic seatours.is.* Whale-watching tours from this small town 30 mins' drive from Akureyri. 99% success rate. Can pick up from your hotel in Akureyri.

Transport

Air

There is a domestic airport in Akureyri, 3 km from the city; buses and taxies run into town. **Air Iceland**, www.airiceland.is, flies to **Reykjavík**'s domestic airport, while **Icelandair**, www.icelandair.is, flies to Keflavík Airport and connects with international flights in summer. There are several flights daily and the journey takes about 45 mins. The private airline, **Norlandair**, www.norlandair.is, has scheduled flights to the island of **Grímsey** daily in summer, 3 times a week in winter, as does **Flugfelag Islands**, www.flugfelag.is.

Boat

To reach the island of **Grímsey** in the Arctic Circle or **Hrisey** by boat, you need to take the **Saefari Ferry**, T458 8970, www.landflutningar.is/saefari, from Dalvik near Akureryi.

The **Eyfor Ferry**, T695 5544, www. hrisey.net, also goes to **Hrisey**, running every 2 hrs from 0700-2300 in the summer, a little less regularly in the winter.

Bus

The coach station is in the centre of Akureyri next to the harbour. There are several daily buses to/from **Reykjavik** taking 6-7 hrs. Buses run between Akureyri and **Húsavík** several times a day from late May to the end of Aug, taking 1 hr 10 mins. Outside this tourist season they run only twice daily. For long-distance bus routes, see www. straeto.is or www.bsi.is. **Sterna** (www. sterna.is) and **SBA Norðurleið** (www. sba.is) run long-distance routes across North Iceland.

Car hire

By car, Akureyri is 389 km from Reykjavík on the ring road. Follow Route 1 under Hvalfjörður, a toll road, and further north until your reach Akureyri; there's little scope to get lost. There are car hire offices at the airport in Akureyri. Companies include **Europcar Iceland**, www.europcar. com, **National**, www.nationalcar.co.uk, and **Thrifty**, www.thrifty.is.

Taxi

Taxi companies in Akureyri include **BSO**, T461 1010, www.bso.is, and **Taxi 17**, T892 4257/896 5318, www.taxi-no17.com.

★Mývatn is the top tourist destination in the area, a beautiful lake broken up with unusual lava formations. The name means 'midge lake' and there are two types of midge that live here, one that likes humans and one that doesn't. They are both essential to the ecosystem around here as there are lots of fish in the water and a massive bird population, including the North American Barrow's goldeneye. The main drop-off point for buses is the village of Reykjahlíð where there is a café, hotel, campsite and souvenir shops.

Around Mývatn

The route to Mývatn from Akureyri takes you past **Góðafoss**, an 11-m-high waterfall whose name means the 'waterfall of the pagan gods'. At the Alþing in AD 1000, Þorgeir, the district commissioner of this area, was the decision maker for whether Iceland should embrace the new Christianity rather than stay faithful to their old pagan gods. He decided that since the Christian god was kind, just and benevolent it would be a better choice than the impetuous and often cruel Norse gods and so Iceland was Christianized. On his return from Þingvellir to the north, he cast his statues of pagan gods into this waterfall.

Around Mývatn itself there are a number of things to see that you can't see anywhere else in the world as a result of the way it has been formed by volcanic activity. The lake itself is 37 sq km but doesn't look that big because it is peppered with islands and birds. Mývatn lies on the boundary of the Eurasian and North American plates and the volcanic activity in the area is ongoing. There is only one real town here, **Reykjahlíð**, where there are a couple of hotels, a campsite and a café-restaurant. Within walking distance of the town you'll find **Grjótagjá**. This was once a popular bathing spot with two caves, one the right temperature and one a little too cold. Volcanic activity in the area has shifted the hot spot so that now the warmer cave is too warm at 60°C but the cold one is just right.

Along the eastern side of the lake you'll find the weird lava formations of the **Dimmuborgir**. These rambling cliffs and scarred pillars of lava are known as the 'dark castles' in Icelandic and you can see why. A pool of molten lava was formed here after an eruption that drained away towards Mývatn and left columns standing behind it, twisted and etched with horizontal lines. Some similar lava shapes were found at the bottom of the sea off the coast of Mexico, but none exist anywhere else on dry land.

There are a huge number of walks to take in the area, mainly clearly marked. Further details can be found in the tourist office at Akureyri where they have a booklet on the area containing walking routes.

Lake Mývatn Nature Baths

Jardbadshólar, 660 Mývatn, T464 4411, www.jardbodin.is. Daily 1200-2200. Jun-Aug ISK 3700, children (12-15s) ISK 1300, concessions ISK 2400, under 12s free; cheaper off season

The Blue Lagoon of the north is set in the mountains near Namaskard, with a naturally heated pool and steam bath offer a relaxing way to spend a morning or afternoon. The lagoon itself is man-made and the water temperature averages 36-40°C. The high concentration of minerals, silicates and geothermal microorganisms is reputed to be particularly beneficial for your skin. Come in the evening, after 2000, at the right time of year and you can watch the Northern Lights while you bathe. You can rent a towel or swimsuit there if you haven't packed one. There is also a small restaurant.

Listings Lake Mývatn

Tourist information

The tourist information centre in Akureyri has information about Lake Mývatn and the surrounding area and there's a commercial tourist centre at Reykjahlíð where you can buy fishing permits, hire bikes, arrange accommodation and buy postcards.

Where to stay

If you have your own transport, staying out of the town around the Mývatn area gives you better access to all the delights of northern Iceland. The website for north Iceland, www.northiceland.is, has a comprehensive listing of all the hotels, B&Bs, campsites and hostels in the area.

€€€€ Hotel Reykjahlid
660 Mývatn, T464 4142, www.myvatnhotel.is.
This rustic 9-room hotel sits on the shore of the lake and has wonderful views as well as a restaurant and lounge. 2 rooms can take an extra bed, making them ideal for small families.

€€€€ Hotel Reynihlíð
Reynihlíð, 660 Mývatn, T464 4170, www.mývatnhotel.is.
The nicer of the 2 small hotels in Reynihlíð with a restaurant, bar and comfortable rooms. Various nature packages are also available, visiting nearby waterfalls and natural wonders.

€€€ Sel Hotel Mývatn
Skútustaðir , 660 Mývatn, T464 4164, www.myvatn.is.
Comfortable 35-roomed hotel close to the Skutustaðagigar pseudo-craters, with plenty of suggestions for active holidays in the area.

€€€-€ Hlid Travel Service
Hraunbrún, 660, Mývatn, T464 4103, www.myvatnaccommodation.is.
Offers a variety of accommodation options, from a guesthouse with 4 double rooms to small private huts, large summer houses with views over the Mývatn area, 9 hotel rooms and a campsite. There's bike rental, horse riding, an information centre and a playground here too. Insect repellent

is essential if you are camping: it's not called 'midge lake' for nothing.

€ Gamli Baerin
Hotel Reynihlíð, 660 Mývatn, T464 4270, www.myvatnhotel.is.
Welcoming café/bar/bistro serving traditional Icelandic food – the likes of lamb soup, smoked arctic char and local beef. Serves coffee and cake too.

What to do

Day tours
Mývatn Tours, *660 Mývatn, T464 1920, www.myvatntours.is.* Day-long guided tours looking at the geology of the Askja caldera and volcanic areas around Mývatn.

Horse riding
Extreme Iceland, *Vatnagarðar 12, 104 Reykjavík, T588 1300, www.extreme*

iceland.is. 8-day riding holidays in the Lake Mývatn area.
Ishestar, *Sorlaskeið 26, 220 Hafnarfjörður, T695 7218, www.ishestar.is.* 8-day tours of the area around Húsavík, Mývatn and Goðafoss and a return to Reykjavík all on horseback.
Saltvik Riding School, *641 Húsavík, T847 9515 (Húsavík), T847 6515 (Mývatn), www.saltvik.is.* Short riding tours of an hour or 2 around Húsavík and Mývatn, plus longer tours if you want.

Swimming
Lake Mývatn Nature Baths,
Jardbadshólar, 660 Mývatn, T464 4411, www.jardbodin.is. Geothermal pool surrounded by the countryside, known as the Blue Lagoon of the north.

Transport

Buses run twice daily to Reykjahlíð from **Akureyri** bus station and there are daily guided coach tours of the area.

Islands of Eyjafjörður

peaceful islands in Iceland's longest fjord

Eyjafjörður is the fjord on which Akureyri is built, and it contains two peaceful islands, Grímsey and Hrísey, which make good half-day trips for families, hikers and birdwatchers. Grímsey is the more popular of the two, offering a chance to visit the Arctic Circle in a day. Day trips or overnight stays can be arranged for both islands.

Grímsey
Grímsey is Iceland's northernmost inhabited island, the home of a fishing community of around a hundred and a bird population of a million. The name means 'stormy' in Icelandic. Its major claim to fame is that it is Iceland's foot in the Arctic Circle, and is about 40 km off the north coast of the country. Sometimes in winter the island is completely surrounded by ice; in the height of summer, there is no night. What to do once you're there? Walk the small 5-km-sq island and marvel at seabirds. Enjoy the solitude. Take a cup of coffee in the only town, Sandvik, and watch the fishermen go about their work. Cross the Arctic Circle and look for polar

bears on the horizon – it has been known for them to come ashore on drift ice from Greenland (although it's very rare). There are a handful of guesthouses on the island so if solitude and very small town life are your thing, you can stay awhile.

Hrísey

Hrísey is a tiny island with walking trails, one cow and around 270 inhabitants. It's actually the biggest island off the coast of Iceland after Heimaey in the Westman Isles and 7.5 km wide at its broadest point. Well-marked walking trails take you around the south of the island but the north has restricted access to protect a colony of breeding eider duck. It's a peaceful and relaxing place to go walking with 40 species of birds, corrugated-iron-clad houses and lots of grassland. Watch out for dive-bombing arctic terns. As you look out towards the eastern mountains of the fjord, look up at the tallest peak, Kaldbakur. It's another of Iceland's powerful new-age energy points. You can also see clearly how the glacier gouged out the fjord. Hrísey also has a guesthouse, swimming pool, church and restaurant and is a great place for a day trip if you like birdwatching, walking and peace and quiet.

Listings Islands of Eyjafjörður

Tourist information

Hrísey Tourist Office
*Norðurvegur 3, T695 0077,
www.hrisey.net or www.visithrisey.is.*

Where to stay

Grímsey

€ Básar
*Básum, 611 Grímsey, T467 3103,
www.gistiheimilidbasar.is.*
The largest of the 2 guesthouses, a warm family-run place offering sleeping-bag accommodation and made-up beds. Lunch and dinner available; the guesthouse also offers sailing trips and sea fishing.

€ Guesthouse Gullsól
*Sólbergi, 611 Grímsey, T467 3190,
gullsol@visir.is.*

Small guesthouse with 6 rooms offering B&B or sleeping bag accommodation. Shared kitchen plus basement boutique selling local Icelandic souvenirs.

Hrísey

€ The Brekka Restaurant
*T466 1751, www.brekkahrisey.is.
Open 15 May-30 Sep.*
Small restaurant with standard B&B accommodation in twin rooms plus sleeping-bag accommodation. Impressive views of the midnight sun.

€ Hrísey Campsite
T461 2255.
Basic campsite perfect for getting back to nature, no mod cons, next to the swimming pool. Open summer only, book in advance.

Restaurants

Hrísey

€ Brekka
IS-630 Hrísey, T695, 3737, www.
brekkahrisey.is. Open 15 May-15 Sep.
The island's only restaurant is and
serves everything from blue mussels
to hamburgers, fish, steak and coffee
and cake.

Transport

Grímsey
Air
There is a domestic airport on Grímsey.
Norlandair, www.norlandair.is, offers
scheduled flights from **Akureyi**, all
year round (daily in summer, otherwise
3 times a week), 30 mins. **Flugfelag
Islands**, www.airiceland.is, offers flights
from both **Akureyri** and **Reykjavík**
domestic airport.

Ferry
To get to Grímsey by boat, you need to
take the **Saefari Ferry**, T458 8970, www.
landflutningar.is/saefari, from Dalvik
near Akureryi. Ferries run 3 times a week
(Mon, Wed and Fri) and take 3 hrs. A
connecting bus from Akureyri, leaving at
0730, is the easiest way to get to the ferry
port at Dalvik. The bus also meets the
incoming ferry in the evening.

Hrísey
Ferry
The **Eyfar Ferry**, T695 5544, www.hrisey.
net, goes to Hrísey from Árskógssandur,
35 km north of Akureyri, every 2 hrs
0700-2300, less frequently in winter. It
takes 15 mins. There is a regular bus trip
from Akureyri to Árskógssandur which
connects with the ferry.

Húsavík

pretty town with a stunning setting; Iceland's whale-watching capital

Húsavík, 91 km from Akureyri on the edge of the next bay along, Skjálfandi, is
a small, pretty fishing town best known for its whale-watching trade. The town
itself is very small with a couple of tourist shops, cafés and guesthouses and
some excellent museums.

Grenjaðarstaður
Stóragarði 17, 640 Húsavík, T464 1860, www.husmus.is. 1 Jun-31 Aug, 1000-1800. ISK 500.

This historic farm site, with its turf-roofed houses, is one of the most historic sites
in the country. Formerly the home of Icelandic chieftains, the site dates back over a
1000 years and was once the most important area in the north of Iceland. Visiting
the farm provides an interesting window on what life was like in this barren
country in years gone by.

Húsavík Church

Jun-Aug 0900-1100 and 1500-1700. Small donation requested.

Built by the first architect of Iceland, this small Norwegian-style church is pretty and overlooks the harbour and dates back to 1907. There has been a church and priest in the town since 1231.

Húsavík Cultural Centre

Stóragarði 17, 640 Húsavík, T464 1860, www.husmus.is. Jun-Aug daily 1000-1800. Sep-May Mon-Fri 0900-1700, Sun 1600-1800.

This lovely museum is the region's main cultural centre and covers all areas of life in northern Iceland from folk tales, natural history and maritime memorabilia to district archives and paintings. Look out for the big polar bear, shot in 1969 on Grímsey, and the weird fish like the deep-sea gulper. It's well worth visiting. The museum shop sells local herbs, crafts and postcards.

Húsavík Whale Museum

Hafnarstétt 1, 640 Húsavík, T414 2800, www.whalemuseum.is. Jun-Aug daily 0830-1830, Apr, May and Sep daily 0900-1600, Oct-Mar Mon-Fri 1000-1200 and 1300-1530. ISK 1400, concessions ISK 1000, children (10-18s) ISK 500, under 10s free.

The Húsavík Whale Museum is a non-profit organization that exists to provide information about whales in Iceland. It's the leading museum of its type in the country and regularly works with the University of Iceland on research projects.

Iceland has quite a sticky relationship with whales and whaling; Húsavík may be one of the world's best places to see whales in their natural habitat, but Iceland's whaling policy has only fairly recently changed to encompass whale watching rather than whaling, and you can still find whale on the menu in a number of Reykjavík restaurants.

This museum has developed in parallel to the country's changing views on whaling: housed in a former slaughter house, it is now the most-visited museum in the north of Iceland, with plenty of anecdotes about whales and Iceland along with beautifully lit skeletons and exhibits. It's a good stop before or after a whale-watching tour (see page 100).

Dettifoss Waterfall

Vatnajökull National Park, www.vatnajokulsthjodgardur.is. Dettifoss is about 1 hr from Húsavík by car. From Húsavík, follow the road 85 northeast and take the road 864 at the 1st junction, after about 60 km. Continue until you reach Dettifoss. Note that road 864 is closed in winter and does not reopen until the end of May. It is possible to visit the waterfall on a guided bus tour on a 'highlights of the north' package, www.sba.is/en.

This magnificent waterfall is said to be the most powerful in Europe and is reachable if you're visiting the north of Iceland. 500 cubic metres of water pass over the falls every second on this 45-m-high, 100-m-wide waterfall. There aren't any facilities to speak of here, just nature in the raw, with a mist of glacial melt water and multiple rainbows lighting in it as you look. Bring waterproofs. For hiking trails in the area, including a 34-km trail from Dettifoss to Asbyrgi, visit the national park website.

Listings Húsavík

Tourist information

The tourist website for northern Iceland, www.nordurthing.is, is a useful resource.

For information contact **Húsavík Whale Museum** (Hafnarstétt 1, T464 4300, www.visithusavik.is).

Where to stay

€€€€ Fosshotel Húsavík
Ketilsbraut 22, 640 Húsavík, T464 1220, www.fosshotel.is.
Small friendly hotel in the centre of town with a restaurant and a beautiful view of the fjord. It's one of the world's few whale-themed hotels, in keeping with the town's main attraction, with a whale stamp collection plus whale-themed books, posters and sculptures. The restaurant is called **Moby Dick**.

€€€ Hotel Rauðaskriða
Rauðaskriða, Aðaldalur, T464 3504, www.hotelraudaskrida.is.
Country hotel on the outskirts of Húsavík with 28 double rooms and a family room sleeping 4-5. Light and bright restaurant and 2 hot tubs with views of the peaceful valley. Also has a summerhouse for hire.

€€€ Kaldbaks-kot Cottages
Kaldbakur, 640 Húsavík, T892 1744, www.husavikcottages.com.
16 log cabins near Húsavík with terraces, views, and private facilities. 1-room cottages through to 4- to 5-bedroom

villas. Stays of 3 nights or more are a little cheaper.

€€ Árból Guest House
Ásgarðsvegur 2, 640 Húsavík, T464 2220, www.arbol.is.
Small, comfortable guesthouse by a stream in the centre of Húsavík. The house dates from 1903 and is warm, romantic and homely.

€ Arbót Youth Hostel
Aðaldalur, T464 3677, www.hostel.is. 1 Jun-15 Sep.
Hostel at a cattle and horse farm in a peaceful valley just outside Húsavík. Has a kitchen, laundry room, dorm rooms and a family room.

€ Húsavík Campground
Héðinsbraut, 640 Húsavík, T464 4300, info@visithusavik.is. 1 Jun-15 Sep.
Simple campsite to the north of the town.

Dettifoss Waterfall

€€€ Skulagarður Country Hotel
Kelduhverfi, T465 2280, www.dettifoss.is. 15 May-15 Sep.
Around 30 mins' drive from Húsavík towards Dettifoss, this small hotel has 17 rooms and offers sleeping-bag accommodation. Has a restaurant and also sells fishing permits. Disabled equipped room.

€ Vesturdalur Campsite
671 Kopasker, T470 7100, www. vatnajokulsthjodgardur.is.

Basic campsite with toilets, showers, washing machine and dryer, snack bar and service station nearby. Resident park rangers offer information.

Restaurants

€ Gamli Baukur
Hafnarstett 9, 640 Húsavík, T464 2442, www.gamlibaukur.is.
Harbourside restaurant serving fresh local seafood and traditional Icelandic food. Also a venue for live music.

€ Salka
Garðarsbraut 6, Húsavík, T464 2551.
Bright airy and spacious restaurant open for lunch and dinner during the week and only for dinner at the weekend. Plenty of seafood and local delicacies to choose from as well as lobster.

What to do

Fishing
Gentle Giants, *Húsavík Harbour, 640 Húsavík, T464 1500, www.gentlegiants.is.* Family company offering sea-fishing trips and whale-watching tours.

Horse riding
Ishestar, *Sorlaskeið 26, 220 Hafnarfjörður, T695 7218, www.ishestar.is.* 8-day tours of the area around Húsavík, Mývatn and Goðafoss and a return to Reykjavík all on horseback.
Saltvík Riding School, *641 Húsavík, T847 9515 (Húsavík), T847 6515 (Mývatn), www.saltvik.is.* Short riding tours of an hour or 2 around Húsavík and Mývatn, plus longer tours if you want.

Skiing
Reykjaheiði Skiing Area, *Húsavíkurfjall, 640 Húsavík, T464 6199, www.volsungur.is/skidi.* Open all year round, particularly for cross-country skiing. Located just outside the town.

Swimming
Húsavík swimming pool, *Laugarbrekka 2, 641 Húsavík, T464 6190. Open year round. ISK 600.* The local municipal thermal pool.

Whale watching
Húsavík is the key location outside Reykjavík for whale watching. Team your trip with a visit to the whale museum to understand how whale watching, whaling and Iceland go together.
Gentle Giants, *see under Fishing, above.*
North Sail, *Gaumli Baukur, Hafnarstett 11, 640 Húsavík, T464 7272, www.northsailing.is.* Whale-watching tours from Húsavík harbour in oak boats with silent diesel engines.

Transport

Bus
Buses run between **Akureyri** and Húsavík several times a day from late May to the end of Aug, taking 1 hr 10 mins. Outside this tourist season they run only twice daily. By car it's a 30-min drive to the north. Long-distance bus routes across the north of Iceland are run by **Sterna** (www.sterna.is) and **SBA Norðurleið** (www.sba.is).

Background
Reykjavík

History

Explorer Pytheas of Massalia reported the discovery of Thule, or Ultima Thule, the northernmost island in the world around 300 BC, six days by sea north of the British Isles. It is unknown whether he was definitely referring to Iceland, but Thule is known to be the oldest name for the country, used in the Middle Ages.

Iceland itself is one of the world's most recently inhabited countries, settled in around AD 874 by Norwegian Viking Ingólfur Arnarson. It is unclear whether he left Norway due to a disagreement with the king or in search of adventure and new territories, but he, his slaves and his compatriots claimed and settled the country and their stories are recorded in the *Book of Settlements* and the *Book of Icelanders*. By AD 930, when the independent Icelandic Commonwealth is established and Alþing parliament was created, the population was around 60,000.

From AD 930-1030, Iceland grew as a nation. Named the Saga Age, this millennium was recorded in texts still read and remembered today. At some time around AD 890, Erik the Red discovered Greenland and he settled there in AD 986.

Iceland became a Christian nation in the year 1000, when the Viking's pagan gods were renounced, officially at least. Pagan worship continued in rural areas and officials turned a blind eye. At around the same time, Icelander Leifur Eiríksson, or Leif Ericson the Lucky, son of Erik the Red, is believed to have discovered America, which he called Vínland.

Iceland settled as a Christian nation in the years 1030-1118 and sustained peace broke out. Later, between 1220 and 1262, the Commonwealth of Iceland was dissolved as Norwegian monarchy grew in power. King Magnus of Norway created a code of law for Iceland, and when his son succeeded the throne at the age of six, he inherited the joint rule of Norway, Iceland and Denmark, bringing the three countries together.

In 1526, the Reformation exerted a huge impact in Denmark, causing a revolt against the king. Christian III became the king and formally establishes the Lutheran church in Iceland, Denmark and the Faroe Islands. In 1662, the King of Denmark, Frederick II, changed the government to become absolute monarch of Iceland, Denmark and Norway.

Reykjavík's fortunes improved in 1749 when Skúli Magnússon became the first Icelandic bailiff. He established workshops and industry in Reykjavík, allowing it to grow beyond a small village. New industries included fishing, agriculture, wool manufacture and mining.

The terrible eruptions of Katla (1755) and Hekla (1766) were topped by the Laki eruptions in spring 1783, lasting a year. They are said to have created the world's largest lava field in historical times by a single eruption. Toxic gas, starvation and the eruption itself reduced the population to about 40,000. Between 9000 and 10,000 people are said to have died from hunger alone.

From 1870 to 1914, between 10,000 and 20,000 Icelanders emigrated to North America, mainly Canada, as persistent earthquakes and volcanoes made farming a desperate game of survival.

ON THE ROAD
Famous Icelanders

Here's a game for you: how many famous Icelanders can you name? It's a little like trying to name more than two famous Belgians, but once you start thinking about it, you'd be surprised how many you have heard of.

Agnar Sverrison
The first Icelander to get a Michelin star, Agnar Sverrison runs **Texture**, a restaurant in London, where fish is always on the menu and butter and cream are banned. His restaurant has scooped Restaurant of the Year awards and accolades from the likes of Raymond Blanc.

Baltasar Kormakur
This Icelandic film director was shortlisted for a Foreign Language Oscar in 2012 for his film *The Deep*, and his newest film *Contraband* stars Mark Wahlberg. Previous films include *101 Reykjavík*, *A Little Trip to Heaven* and *Jar City*.

Björk
If you don't know anyone else, you'll know her. This quirky songstress had several top-10 singles in the 1990s, has been nominated for 13 Grammy awards and won the Best Actress Award at the Cannes Film Festival in 2000. She lives in New York with artist Matthew Barney.

Bobby Fischer
American Chess Grandmaster Bobby Fischer was granted Icelandic citizenship in 2005. He is famed for winning the World Championship from Boris Spassky of the USSR in 1972, at the height of the Cold War, in a match held in Reykjavík.

The year 1874 marked a millennium of settlement. The Danish king brought a constitution for the country for the celebration allowing legislative and financial power to rest with the Alþing but all laws still had to be signed by the king himself. In 1904, executive power of the government was transferred from Copenhagen to Reykjavík and by 1918, Iceland was granted freedom as a sovereign state of Denmark in the Act of Union.

The British occupied Iceland peacefully during the Second World War as a strategic location in the middle of the North Atlantic. Later the Americans replaced the British.

Iceland was proclaimed a republic on 17 June 1944 after political changes in Denmark as a result of the Second World War. Independence is celebrated on this day every year.

In 1945, the Keflavík Treaty was agreed allowing the USA to lease the strategically important military base in Keflavík for a period of 99 years.

Iceland gained membership to NATO in 1949.

Between 1952 and 1977, the Cod Wars were waged with Britain, Germany and other nations fishing in the North Atlantic to preserve Icelandic fishing waters. Iceland was victorious.

Erik the Red

This Viking explorer and Norwegian outlaw was probably called 'the red' because of his hair. He founded the first colony in Greenland after being exiled to Iceland from Norway following a blood feud.

Halldor Laxness

This 20th-century Icelandic writer won the Nobel Prize for Literature in 1955 for his novel *Independent People*, all about the poverty and struggle of rural life in his country. He is the only Icelandic Nobel Laureate and his works have been widely translated.

Jónsi

Sigur Rós are the other big music act you'll likely have heard of. Their lead singer, Jónsi, has put out solo material. He sings in a combination of Icelandic and English that he calls Hopelandic and plays the guitar with a bow.

Leif Eriksson

Back in the year 1000 AD, Leif (Leifur Eiriksson to give him his Icelandic name) was the first man to discover America. The son of Erik the Red (above), he was a Viking explorer and the Norse settlement he founded, called Vinland, is thought to be in Newfoundland in modern-day Canada. There's a statue of him in St Paul, Minnesota, as well as outside the Hallgrimskirkja in Reykjavík.

Magnus Magnusson

The father of TV show *Mastermind* was born in Iceland but lived in Scotland for most of his life. He worked as a TV journalist before becoming the presenter of the TV quiz. He also translated a number of ancient and modern books into English from Icelandic.

The World Chess Championships took place in Reykjavík in 1972 between American Bobby Fischer and Russian Boris Spassky. Fischer won and it was hailed a Cold War victory and one of the greatest games of chess ever played.

In 1980 Vigdís Finnbogadóttir became the President of Iceland, the first female and single mother to become a president anywhere in the world.

Iceland declared itself a nuclear-free zone in 1985.

In 2008, Iceland suffered the largest banking crisis suffered by any country in economic history, with the collapse of its three major banks. The country narrowly escaped total bankruptcy and suffered a major recession for the following four years, kick starting economic problems the world over.

In 2010 the volcano Eyjafjallajökull erupted on the south coast of Iceland, stopping air traffic around the world with a giant ash cloud.

Today Reykjavík is a modern capital city, with major interests in tourism. Although the recession is still being felt in parts, new buildings such as the Harpa concert hall and innovative tourist activities are pointing towards a brighter future.

Practicalities
Reykjavík

Getting there

Iceland's only international airport, **Keflavik Airport**, is 50 km from the city. **Icelandair** ⓘ *www.icelandair.com*, **Air Iceland** ⓘ *www.airiceland.com*, **easyJet** ⓘ *www.easyjet.com*, and budget airline **WOW Air** ⓘ *www.wowiceland.co.uk*, run flights from Europe all year round. From March to June there are additional summer services with an array of European budget airlines covering most major European cities. From the USA, **Icelandair** flights are available from a number of major cities including Boston and Seattle. Other long-haul international flights connect in London.

The route from the airport to Reykjavík is easy and takes just under an hour. The cheapest way to travel is via **Flybus** ⓘ *www.re.is/flybus*, or **Airport Express** ⓘ *www.airportexpress.is*, coach services running from outside the terminal to the city centre and various hotels. Return tickets cost ISK 4400. As the route to the airport passes close to the Blue Lagoon, it's a convenient place to visit before flying home; there are numerous options that will take you there (see page 64). Taxis are available outside Arrivals and cost approximately ISK 16,500 to reach central Reykjavík. There are also car hire desks in Arrivals though car hire tends to be cheaper when booked in advance. ▸▸ *See Transport, page 61.*

Getting around

Most of Reykjavík's cultural sights and attractions are in the 101 district (Old Town), which is in easy walking distance of most of the major hotels and B&Bs and is a lovely place to spend an afternoon or two. There is no train service in Iceland; the city is served by reliable buses, but the chances are you won't need to use them. **Bikecompany.is** rents bikes in the city, a good way to get around, and runs cycling tours in and beyond it. Taxis are metered and reliable but fiendishly expensive, costing around ISK 20,000 for 4 km. There is a taxi rank beside the tourist information office in the Old Town and another on Lækjartorg.

The major natural attractions, including Þingvellir National Park, Geysir and Gullfoss waterfall, are a drive away, and those wanting to experience glaciers, snowmobiling or other winter sports will also have to take a trip out of the city. This can be arranged via the many tour offices in the city, most of whom run day tours by bus, jeep or car from the city, with pick-up from your hotel. Coaches from the central **BSÍ** bus station link the city with other Icelandic destinations.

You can do all of the above under your own steam too, with a hire car. There are car rental offices at Keflavik Airport and in the centre of the city. Parking is easy on the street, although you may have to pay a little at a meter in central areas. When driving outside the city, be sure to take a map as well as GPS as the signal is not 100% reliable in all regions, and obey all traffic laws. Iceland's weather is notorious for sweeping in suddenly and causing chaos. Some of the roads in the highlands region are only open in the summer months. Check **Vegagerðin** ⓘ *www.vegagerdin.is*, for details of road closures throughout the country. **Samferda** ⓘ *www.samferda.is*, is a useful site which helps travellers arrange carpooling, to save on the costs of car rental and fuel. ▸▸ *See also Transport, page 61.*

Tour operators and self-drive tours

There are lots of non-Icelandic tour operators going to Iceland, many of which have been operating for several years. The better ones can arrange tailor-made tours and organize extensions to Greenland and beyond. These are worth checking out as they can represent good value especially if you are going for a limited time. If you are hoping to explore beyond Reykjavik, self-drive tours of Iceland are a popular alternative to simply hiring a car at the airport. Companies such as **Discover the World** ⓘ *T01737-214291(UK), www.discover-the-world.co.uk/ Iceland*, will loan out a digital travel app set up with personal itineraries to guide travellers around the country's top sites as well as its hidden gems. Discover the World also organize Northern Lights adventures, wildlife watching, hiking and exploring in small groups with award-winning guides.

Essentials A-Z

Accident and emergency

General emergencies: 112.
This universal emergency number covers **Police**, **Fire Brigade**, **Ambulance** and **Rescue** services. **Non-urgent police**: T444 1000.

Customs and duty free

Travellers may import 1 litre of spirits, 1 litre of wine and 200 cigarettes or 250 g cigars or tobacco. Various variations are approved: 1 litre of spirits, 6 litres of beer and 200 cigarettes are permitted, as are 1.5 litres of wine, 6 litres of beer and 200 cigarettes and 3 litres of wine and 200 cigarettes. The minimum age for bringing in alcohol is 20 and for tobacco it is 18.

Angling and riding gear must be fully disinfected before reaching Iceland to protect native species. If in doubt, contact the **Icelandic Customs Authority**, T569 1750, www.tollur.is.

Disabled travellers

Iceland is relatively disabled friendly with plenty of wheelchair accessible hotels and attractions – including Þingvellir National Park, Geysir and a number of hot springs and local swimming pools.

Within the city, **Reykjavík Group Travel Service**, T587 8030, www.randburg.com/is, has 2 coaches specially designed for wheelchairs and they also organize tours for the disabled in Iceland.

Car rental firm **Hertz**, T522 4400, offers a specially fitted car for wheelchair users.

And the tourist information office on Aðalstræti can provide further information on disabled travel in the country (see page 39).

Electricity

220 volts, 50 Hz AC. Appliances use a standard European 2-pin plug.

Embassies and consulates

For all Icelandic embassies and consulates abroad and for all foreign embassies and consulates in Reykjavík, see http://embassy.goabroad.com.

Health

Medical facilities in Reykjavík are very good. EU citizens should make sure they have the **European Health Insurance Card** (**EHIC**), which provides reciprocal rights to medical care. They are available free of charge in the UK from the **Department of Health**, www.dh.gov.uk, or post offices.

Non-EU citizens should ensure their travel insurance covers emergency and routine medical needs, particularly if you are likely to take part in any sports or activities. You may need to check that winter sports cover is included. Check for reciprocal cover with your private or public health scheme first. Should you encounter difficulties or emergencies in areas outside Reykjavík you may require helicopter assistance.

Travellers do not require any vaccinations for visiting Iceland.

Water is safe to drink from any source – ie straight from the tap or from local streams or water fountains. Hot water has a strange smell of sulphur but is not harmful.

The biggest challenges to health in Iceland are weather and risky behaviour in unpredictable terrain. See Safety, below.

Medical services

There is a 24-hr casualty department at the **National University Hospital**, T543 1000 and at the **Fossvogur Landspítali Háskólasjúkrahús Hospital**, 108 Reykjavík, T525 1700. **Akureyri Hospital** is the best-equipped emergency hospital outside Reykjavík. **Sjúkrahús Akureyrar**, Eyrarlandsvegur, 600 Akureyri, T463 0100. Reykjavík has several pharmacies (*apotek*), 2 of which are open daily 0800-2400. For **dentists** on duty, call T575 0505. There is a **health centre** for tourists, T510 6500, www.hv.is.

Insurance

It is recommended that you take out insurance before travelling without insurance is not recommended. In the event of theft, contact the **Reykjavík police station**, T444 2500, Skulugata 21. See also Health, above.

Internet

Most Reykjavík cafés offer free Wi-Fi; the tourist information centre at Aðalstræti 2 has internet access for a small fee. Most hotels also have Wi-Fi.

Language

It is rare to find an Icelander under 50 who doesn't speak perfect English, particularly in Reykjavík. Tourist information is primarily in English and nobody blinks an eyelid at you for speaking it. The language shares a common root with English but is utterly distinguishable from it, with plenty of unique sounds and a singsong style. Probably the most well-known feature of its language is the patronymic naming system, where men have the affix *–són* (son) and women – *dóttir* (daughter) added to their father's first name to create a surname, hence Björk Guðmundsdóttir – Guðmund's daughter.

Language schools

There is not much call for learning Icelandic, but if you are interested in the language, the University of Iceland's language centre offers a beginner's online course in the language as well as an undergraduate course: www.ask.hi.is/page/learningicelandic.

Money

→ *£1 = ISK 205, €1 = ISK 148, US$1 = ISK 131 (May 2015). For up-to-the-minute exchange rates, visit www.xe.com.*

ATMs and banks

The best way to get money in Reykjavík is with a credit or debit card. There are ATM machines in the Arrivals hall at the airport, and in several banks in the centre of the city.

Banks are usually open Mon-Fri 0915-1600. All banks change foreign exchange.

Cost of living

Iceland is one of the most expensive cities in the world, based on comparing global average prices for basic goods. Some of this is simply because of economies of scale and geography – Iceland has a small population, has to fly many goods in and has a limited manufacturing industry.

TRAVEL TIP
On a budget

Reykjavík may no longer be the most expensive city in the world, but don't be fooled. The country's economic collapse has not created a cheap place to be – so here are some tips for travellers on a budget.

Accommodation Iceland is pricey and there aren't many hotels on the cheap side. Consider booking into one of Reykjavík's brilliant youth hostels or camping in the summer to keep costs low. There are also plenty of apartments to rent and if you're holidaying with a group or family, they can work out as really good value, especially as you won't have to eat out for every meal.

Eating There are some cheap eats to look out for and some great cafés that will fill you up without costing the earth. Look out particularly for the local hot dog stalls which are a real snip. Some shops also offer free coffee when you're browsing, particularly in the winter. Bonus and Kronan are the lowest priced supermarkets if you're self catering. Icelandic water is fine to drink from the tap – don't bother buying bottled water.

Reykjavík Welcome Card This tourist card offers you access to major museums, thermal swimming pools and bus transport as well as discounts in various shops and restaurants and free internet access. It costs ISK 3300 for 24 hours, ISK 4400 for 48 hours and ISK 4900 for 72 hours. Buy it at the tourist information centre, Icelandic Travel Market, Trip.is, Reykjavík City Hostel, Downtown Hostel, Hlemmur bus station, Reykjavík Campsite, Reykjavík Art Museum or Reykjavík Backpackers Hostel.

Souvenirs Head to the Kolaportið market at the weekend down by the harbour for the best value souvenirs in the city. You can find Icelandic *lopi* jumpers for half the price of the tourist shops and can try a square of *hákarl* or rotten shark for free at the fishmongers. Trust me, you'll be glad you didn't pay for it.

You can claim tax back as part of the country's tax free scheme if you buy products costing more than ISK 4000, so always ask for your receipt and collect your refund at the airport or at the tourist information centre on departure.

Swimming pools For just ISK 650 you can spend a happy few hours floating in thermal water in one of Reykjavík's swimming pools. There are several in the city; Laugardalslaug is the best overall, with an outdoor pool, hot tubs and a slide.

Transport You don't need a car if you're just visiting the city for a few days – as petrol is expensive, this will keep your costs down. Travel from the airport by airport bus – don't even think about a taxi, which can cost a fortune – and get around the city on foot. There are plenty of day tour companies that can take you out to see the natural sights around the city, so you don't need a car; of course, if you're a family or group, it might work out cheaper to pool resources and hire one. The youth hostels are a good place to find someone who might want to share if you're travelling solo.

Alcohol is particularly expensive; cut your costs by buying local. Recognizable imports like Heineken beer are likely to be a lot more expensive than the local brews.

While travel in the shoulder seasons of spring and autumn may be a little cheaper, you do lose out on the extreme phenomena – the Northern Lights and the midnight sun – so there is a reason for the lower prices.

Backpackers can make use of the great Icelandic hostel network, or otherwise camp. Some B&Bs offer 'sleeping bag accommodation' – a put-me-up bed that you stay in if you bring a sleeping bag, which can help cut costs, and beyond the capital, rural schools are often turned into cheap youth hostels/hotels in the summer months and are worth looking out for.

Public transport is cheap, but if you're staying in the city, the most cost-conscious way to get around is on foot. Car hire and petrol can be expensive, and bus tours are an alternative way to see the natural sights beyond the city.

If you're looking for a budget-conscious way to see the city, get a **Reykjavík Welcome Card** (see previous page), offering free entry to museums and galleries, bus travel and extras, and be sure to check out the local thermal swimming pools. For a handful of coins you can enjoy the Icelandic ritual of swimming in geothermally heated water.

Currency and exchange
The Icelandic currency is the Icelandic krona (ISK or Kr). Coins come in denominations of 1, 5, 10, 50 and 100 while notes come in denominations of 500, 1000, 2000 and 5000.

The coins offer a lovely flavour of the country – each one has a different fish on it.

Opening hours

Banks: Mon-Fri 0915-1600.
Business hours: Mon-Fri 1000-1800.
Post office: Mon-Fri 0900-1800.
Shops: Mon-Fri 1000-1800, Sat 1000-1600. Many shops are closed on Sun except for bakeries, florists, souvenir shops and bookshops.

Post

The main post office is on Pósthússtræti and is a large red building with the words 'Icelandspóstur' on it.

Post boxes are yellow with a horn on them. Post is fairly efficient with delivery times to Western Europe at around 2-4 days.

Safety

Reykjavík is a relatively safe city to visit with low levels of crime and violence. That said, petty theft occurs at swimming pools – hand your valuables into the desk before changing – and it's not uncommon to occasionally see brawls on a Fri or Sat night in the city centre. Pickpockets and violent crime are not common.

The main safety risks in the country come from risky behaviour in unpredictable terrain and the weather. Always let people know where you're going and when you expect to arrive and check weather before leaving. Be sure to check www.safetravel.is before you visit if you are planning to embark on any hikes or adventure activities outside the city without a guide – it contains information about weather, routes, equipment lists and planning trips. If you are planning to walk in a recently active volcanic area, take a guide or make use of local knowledge. Take a map when driving, as GPS can be unreliable in central areas of the highlands, and be sure that you understand local traffic laws.

Smoking

Smoking is prohibited in public areas in Iceland. This includes all public transport and all restaurants, bars and cafés.

Student travellers

The **International Student Identity Card (ISIC)** for full time students can help you access discounts on transport and attractions in Iceland, as can a valid student identity card.

Tax

Iceland, like many Scandinavian countries, has steep taxes and most goods and services are subject to 7-15% value added tax. VAT is included in prices. If you are a non-Icelandic citizen, you can claim a tax rebate on exiting the country. Those spending over ISK 4000 in one shop can claim a tax rebate. Ask for a tax-free form in the shop, which allows you to claim 7-15% back. Services and food are excluded. There is a tax-free booth in Keflavik Airport as well as various other locations in the city.

Telephone → *Country code: 00354.*

There are few on-street telephone booths as Iceland has a high proportion of mobile phone users. You can buy local pay-as-you-go SIM cards at the tourist information centre at Keflavik Airport.

Prepaid calling cards for public phones are available at the post office.

If looking up Icelanders in the phone book, search under their given name, not their family name ie look under B for Björk.

Time

Greenwich Mean Time year round.

Tipping

Tipping is not expected or solicited.

Tourist information

The official website www.visitreykjavik.is is an essential read before touching down in the city, offering advice, weather forecasts and booking services as well as swift replies to queries on email. They also have internet access.

The main office is at Aðalstræti 2 in the centre of the city (see page 39). There is also a small concession in Keflavik Airport.

Visas and immigration

Visas are not typically required for visitors from the EU, Australia and North America for stays of up to 90 days. Australia, Canadian and American nationals may need to have a return ticket to enter; EU and UK nationals can enter without one. Passport validity must be at least 3 months beyond the intended length of stay, and 6 months is recommended, if you are not an EU citizen. For more information consult www.utl.is.

Weights and measures

Metric.

Notes

Index → Entries in **bold** refer to maps

FOOTPRINT
Features

About the author

Laura Dixon is an established travel writer who has been writing about Iceland for over 15 years. She wrote Footprint's first guide to the city of Reykjavík and has been updating it ever since, as the country weathered a financial crisis, a volcanic eruption and saw questions develop about its role in Europe and its relationship with the environment. She likes nothing more than swimming in hot springs and feasting on Nizza chocolate and licorice bars. As for Hakarl, *nei takk*. Her wildest adventures in Iceland have involved partying in the midnight sun, chasing the Northern Lights and polar bear hunting. She lives with her family in the UK and returns to Reykjavík as often as she can.

Price codes

Where to stay	
€€€€	over €300
€€€	€200-300
€€	€100-200
€	under €100

Based on the cost of two people sharing a double room in high season.

Restaurants	
€€€	over €30
€€	€15-30
€	under €15

Price refers to the cost of a two-course meal for one person, including drinks and service charge.

Credits

Footprint credits
Editor: Nicola Gibbs
Production and layout: Emma Bryers
Maps: Kevin Feeney
Colour section: Angus Dawson

Publisher: Patrick Dawson
Managing Editor: Felicity Laughton
Administration: Elizabeth Taylor
Advertising sales and marketing:
John Sadler, Kirsty Holmes,
Debbie Wylde

Photography credits
Front cover: Seth Resnick/SuperStock
Back cover: Top: Jamen Percy/
Shutterstock.com.
Bottom: Pyty/Shutterstock.com

Colour section
Inside front cover: Vadim Petrakov/
Shutterstock.com, Radius/SuperStock,
Mikel Bilbao/SuperStock.
Page 1: Felix Lipov/Shutterstock.com.
Page 2: Mliberra/Shutterstock.com.
Page 4: Danuta Hyniewska/SuperStock.
Page 5: kan_khampanya/Shutterstock.
com, Sergemi/Shutterstock.com,
leospek/Shutterstock.com, Solodov
Alexey/Shutterstock.com.
Page 6: Santi Román/SuperStock.
Page 7: Art Wolfe Stock/SuperStock,
Filip Fuxa/Shutterstock.com.
Page 8: Tsuguliev/Shutterstock.com.

Printed in Spain by GraphyCems

Publishing information
Footprint Reykjavík
2nd edition
© Footprint Handbooks Ltd
July 2015

ISBN: 978 1 910120 52 1
CIP DATA: A catalogue record for this
book is available from the British Library

® Footprint Handbooks and the
Footprint mark are a registered
trademark of Footprint Handbooks Ltd

Published by Footprint
6 Riverside Court
Lower Bristol Road
Bath BA2 3DZ, UK
T +44 (0)1225 469141
F +44 (0)1225 469461
footprinttravelguides.com

Distributed in the USA by
National Book Network, Inc.

Every effort has been made to ensure
that the facts in this guidebook are
accurate. However, travellers should still
obtain advice from consulates, airlines,
etc about travel and visa requirements
before travelling. The authors and
publishers cannot accept responsibility
for any loss, injury or inconvenience
however caused.